SING
DANCE
SHOUT!

SING DANCE SHOUT!

30 Days of Praise

DORAINE BENNETT

CF4•K

10 9 8 7 6 5 4 3 2 1
© Copyright 2011 Doraine Bennett
ISBN: 978-1-84550-656-8

Published by Christian Focus Publications
Geanies House, Fearn, Tain, Ross-shire,
IV20 1TW, Scotland, U.K.
www.christianfocus.com
email: info@christianfocus.com

Cover design by moose77.com
Illustrations by Kim Shaw
Printed and bound by Bell and Bain, Glasgow

Mixed Sources
Product group from well-managed
forests and other controlled sources
www.fsc.org Cert no.TT-COC-002769
© 1996 Forest Stewardship Council

CONTENTS

1. WHAT IS PRAISE?

Praise our God, O peoples, let the sound of his praise be heard (Psalm 66:8).

"Cool shirt, man."

"New haircut? It looks great."

"I'm so proud of you."

"Two goals in one game! That's amazing."

"Good work on your report. It deserves an A+."

Has anyone ever said words like these to you? Didn't they make you feel good? Didn't you love hearing them? That's what praise is all about. Whether you're talking about a great soccer goal, a new outfit, or a kind act, you offer praise when you tell someone how much you like something about them. You praise them when you admire something they have done. You do it all the time.

In this book, you'll learn about praise as it relates to God. In praise, you tell God how much you love him and why. Praise focuses on who God is. You praise him for his character. He is faithful, just, loving, and holy. You tell him what an awesome God he is. You thank him for what he has done. He cares for you, provides for you, and loves you. He created you and knows everything about you. He knows what you're good at and what you struggle with. He knows the secrets in your heart. He is always on your side. Praise expresses your love and your gratitude for these things.

It's important to remember that praise is "expressed." It isn't silent. It's excited and proud. If you score a goal at your soccer game, you want your teammates to give you a high five, or shout your name and say, "Way to go!" What would their praise accomplish if they only sat and thought about what a great kick you made? You wouldn't know how they felt. Praise must be expressed to work.

The Hebrew people were emotional and vocal in their praise to God. They sang, shouted, and lifted their hands. They played instruments and danced. They praised God when they saw his wonders and when they experienced his deliverance. They even praised when they were sad.

Praise doesn't depend on how you feel. The Old Testament worshippers understood that. They called it the sacrifice of praise. Their praise was an offering to God, an offering they made based on how wonderful God was and is and always will be.

God wants you to praise him. He wants you to praise when you feel good. He wants you to praise when you feel lousy. He wants you to praise when you wake up in the morning and when you go to bed at night and in between. He wants you to praise when you're alone and when you're with your friends and family.

You can praise anywhere. In your room or on your bike, at the playground or in the car. Some people have a special place where they like to spend time with God. It could be a chair in your room or in the shade beneath a tree. You might want to find a private place while you're working your way through the praise projects in the following chapters. Find a place where you can be alone with

God. Each praise project will give you a chance to experiment with the many ways people in the Bible expressed their praise to God. Get comfortable praising God in private, then move on to praising him with your family and friends.

Praise Project

Find a quiet place. Tell God that you want to learn to praise him. Ask him to help you. He will.

Read Psalm 66 in your Bible.

The first verse says this: Shout with joy to God, all the earth! Sing the glory of his name; make his praise glorious! Say to God, "How awesome are your deeds! So great is your power that your enemies cringe before you. All the earth bows down to you; they sing praises to you, they sing praise to your name."

The psalm writer tells you exactly what to say to God. Try praising God with his words. Then see if you can find words of your own to praise God.

2. What Happens When You Praise?

Yet you are holy, enthroned on the praises of Israel (Psalm 22:3 ESV).

An odd thing happens when someone praises you. You feel connected to that person. Someone has taken the time to notice you and to tell you so. It makes you want to spend more time around them. Just the opposite happens when someone criticizes you. You don't want to be around that person any more. But praise draws you in. It brings you close. It creates and deepens a relationship.

Your parents may praise you for doing your chores well or being kind to your younger sister. Your teacher may praise you for studying hard and making good grades. Your coach may praise you for trying hard in a ball game. A friend may praise your new dress. Praise is like water to a wilting plant. It lifts your spirit and brightens your day.

We don't praise God in order to lift his spirits. God doesn't need our praises for that reason. In fact, he doesn't *need* our praises at all. But God understands the connection that praise creates. He knows that as you praise him, you will begin to sense your connection to him. That's why God loves your praises. He loves to be where people are praising him. The Bible says praising God is like building a throne for him to come and sit. God comes and sits down and enjoys your praise.

Praise is not just for God's sake. It has great benefits for you, the one who praises. Praise can help you see the difficult things in your life from God's perspective. Sometimes problems can seem insurmountable. They seem too big to do anything about. Remember the story of Zacchaeus? He was short, and he was stuck in the crowd. He couldn't see Jesus, so he climbed a sycamore tree. Praising God is like you climbing your own sycamore tree. You get up above your struggles and worries, and you find that you can see Jesus. You can see your problems from his point of view. You can see that God is bigger than all of your struggles. Praise gives you hope and faith that there is a solution.

Because praise is spoken, it actually increases your faith. The Bible says that faith comes by hearing, hearing the truth of God's word. In praise, you declare out loud how good God is, how awesome he is, how much he loves you, how faithful he is. The words leave your mouth and enter your ears. They go down into your very heart and take root. And faith grows!

And finally, praise frightens your enemy, the devil. The Bible says the devil is like a roaring lion that wants to devour you. He wants to steal your joy, kill your hope, and make you a slave to anger. He wants to destroy your future. When you speak Jesus' name, the devil trembles. Praise is a good way to keep him away.

As you praise, you will begin to sense God's presence around you. You can watch your faith grow. You'll see the enemy leave you alone. Climb up the sycamore tree of praise, just like Zacchaeus did, and ask God to let you see your life the way he sees it.

Praise Project

Remember a time when someone praised you. Remember how it made you feel. Tell God that you want to create a special connection to him with your praise. Remind him of his promise to come and sit down with you and listen to your praise.

Can you think of ways to praise God? What can you say to him that would be like a compliment? You might want to make a list if it helps you to think of good things you can say about God. Once you have made your list, read it aloud to him. Remember, praise must be expressed to work.

3. Yadah:

TO THROW UP YOUR HANDS IN POWER

"I will praise you, O LORD, with all my heart; I will tell of all your wonders" (Psalm 9:1).

David was about fifteen years old when his father sent him to deliver cheese and bread to his brothers who were fighting against the Philistines. The army of Israel was on one hillside. The army of the Philistines was on another, with a valley between them.

Every morning and every evening for forty days, Goliath the giant walked into the valley. He stood nearly ten feet tall. His spear was as big as a fence rail.

He shouted at Saul's army. "Pick your best fighter and let him fight with me. If he wins, then we will be your slaves. But if I win, you will be our slaves."

The Israelites trembled at the dare. They looked at one another and shook their heads.

When David arrived at the camp, he heard Goliath's threats.

"I defy the armies of Israel!" the giant shouted.

"Who does he think he is?" David asked. "He can't talk like that to the army of God!" David was offended. He knew no one should be talking like that about the Almighty God of Israel.

David's brothers thought he was showing off. King Saul thought he was just a scrawny kid. David told them how he killed the lion and the bear that tried to take his father's sheep. "I'll do the same to this Philistine dog who thinks he can taunt the army of God," David said.

So they let him go down into the valley.

David took his sling and five smooth stones.

Goliath laughed. "I'll turn you into food for the buzzards."

David felt the stones in his pocket. "You come to me with a sword and a shield, but I come in the name of the LORD Almighty. I'm going to kill you and cut off your head. Then everyone will know there's a mighty God in Israel." David remembered the lion and the bear. He walked closer to Goliath. "God doesn't save us with a spear," he shouted. "The battle is the LORD's, and he will give all of you into our hands!"

The angry Philistine started down the hill toward David to kill him.

David took off. He ran right at Goliath. He reached into his pocket, grabbed a stone, and placed it in his sling. He swung the leather sling around in the air and let go of the cord. The stone hit Goliath square in the forehead. The giant crashed down into the dirt.

When the Philistines saw their champion was dead, they ran for their lives.

The battle was won.

Some people believe David was thinking about his battle with Goliath when he wrote Psalm 9. No one knows for sure, but there is an interesting connection between the story and the psalm. Psalm 9:1 says, "I will praise you, O LORD, with all my heart." The word David used for praise in this verse means to throw up your hands in power. Picture in your mind the motion David used to throw his sling. It would be the same type of motion you use to throw a ball. You extend your arm out in front of you with your hand open. It takes power to throw a sling or a ball and make it go very far, so it's not a gentle movement. In the psalm, David isn't throwing a rock from a sling. He's throwing praise, and he's throwing it with all his might.

Just as God helped David defeat Goliath, God helps you defeat the giants you face. They might not be real flesh and blood giants like Goliath. God helps you defeat fear, shyness, and anger. He helps you defeat bad habits. He helps you to fight against selfishness. Those things can be like giants in your life. Be like David and throw your praise to Him with all your might.

Praise Project

Find a ball or roll up a piece of paper into a wad. Throw it and watch the motion your arm and hand makes. That motion is a *yadah*. Now read Psalm 9:1 several times. Say it aloud until you can remember it without looking at the page. Add the *yadah*, your lifted hand.

I will praise you (*yadah*), O LORD, with all my heart (*yadah*).

I will tell (*yadah*) of all your wonders (*yadah*).

4. Halal:

TO BOAST IN THE CONGREGATION

Praise ye the LORD. I will praise the LORD with my whole heart, in the assembly of the upright, and in the congregation (Psalm 111:1 KJV).

Absalom was one handsome guy. In all of Israel there was no one so highly praised for his good looks. He had great hair. He was something to look at. He loved listening to all the grand things people said about him. He agreed with all of them. He thought he was something special. In fact, he thought he was so special that he should be king instead of his dad, David. He wanted to be king, so he began to plot.

He started riding through town in his fancy horse-drawn chariot with fifty men running in front of him. He wanted everyone to think he was rich and powerful. He parked by the city gate every morning. When anyone came through the gates on their way to see the King, Absalom called them over. He pretended to listen to their problems. He acted like they were important, but that's what it was – an act. It was part of the plot.

"Where are you from?" Absalom would ask. "Look, you've got a strong case, but the king isn't going to listen to you. Why doesn't somebody make me the judge? I'd make sure all your problems were settled fair and square."

If anyone came and tried to bow down to him, he grabbed them by the hand and pulled them to their feet and greeted them just like they were an equal with the king's son. The people of Israel loved him for it. They didn't know Absalom was plotting to take over.

After several years of this, Absalom took a trip. His plot was nearly complete. When he arrived at Hebron, he sent secret messengers throughout all Israel. "Whenever you hear the sound of the trumpets, then say: Absalom is king in Hebron!"

The trumpet sounded, and Absalom proclaimed himself king.

Absalom's victory didn't last long. When David heard the news, he left Jerusalem, but he sent men faithful to him back to the city. They would try to give Absalom bad advice, in hope that he would listen to them and make mistakes. And that's just what happened.

Absalom decided to enjoy his triumph. He sat on the throne and ate in the palace instead of going after David and his army. This gave David time to organize his army and make battle plans. David's friends from all over Israel came to join him. They wouldn't let David go with them into battle. They didn't want the true king to be hurt.

The armies met in a forest near the Jordan River and fought a battle. David's army won a great victory. When Absalom realized the battle was lost, he rode off. He raced through the low branches of the forest hoping to escape, but his beautiful, long hair caught in a tree. He hung there until one of David's soldiers came along and killed him. You can read the whole story in 2 Samuel 15-19.

The people praised Absalom for his beauty. This word for *praise* is *halal*. It's a Hebrew word that means *to boast* or *to brag*. The people bragged about Absalom. Absalom bragged about himself. He bragged about the wrong things.

What do you brag about? Is it the way you look, how smart you are, or how many goals you can score? Do you know what the Bible tells us to brag about? "This is what the LORD says: Let not the wise man boast of his wisdom or the strong man boast of his strength or the rich man boast of his riches, but let him who boasts boast about this: that he understands and knows me, that I am the LORD," Jeremiah 9:23-24.

So bragging about God is a good thing. In fact, that's exactly what David meant when he said, "Praise ye the LORD!" It's that same word, *halal*. Here it means to brag on God, to say how wonderful He is.

David says he's going to brag on God with all his heart. He's going to brag in private and brag in public. He's going to brag when there are just a few people around and when the whole church is gathered together. He's going to stand up and say: Hallelujah! Can you guess where that word comes from? *Hallel* means to boast. *Jah* is the short way to write Jehovah, the proper name for the one true God. Put them together and you have a great big boast about God.

Praise Project

Use the alphabet to name things about God that you can brag on. Make it a group project with your family or your class, and let each person take a letter in turn as you move around the group. You might have to give yourself a little room on the letter x. Try a word beginning with ex, like exalted or exciting.

Try it once bragging about God, Jesus or the Holy Spirit:

*God is **A**wesome. Hallelujah!*

*Jesus is **B**eautiful. Hallelujah!*

*The Holy Spirit is **C**aring. Hallelujah!*

Now try it again. This time brag directly to the Lord.

*God, you are **a**wesome.*

*Jesus, you are **b**eautiful.*

*Holy Spirit, you are so **c**aring.*

Praise God. Hallelujah!

Remember. Praise with your whole heart. Hallelujah!

5. Gadal:

TO MAGNIFY

O magnify the LORD with me, and let us exalt his name together (Psalm 34:3 NKJV).

One day an angel came to visit a young woman named Mary. The angel told her she would be the mother of Jesus. Mary must have been very surprised. She must not have understood everything that was happening to her, but she believed God.

Soon after the angel came, Mary went to visit her cousin Elizabeth. Elizabeth was expecting a baby too. The two women had not seen each other in a long while. Mary opened the gate and walked into Elizabeth's home.

Elizabeth looked up from her work. The baby inside her jumped for joy. She sang out her greeting to Mary. "Blessed are you among women!" Elizabeth knew there was something special about Mary's baby. She knew the baby was from God.

Mary answered, "My soul magnifies the Lord! My spirit rejoices!"

Maybe they hugged and danced around the room together. They were celebrating something amazing. God was sending His son into the world as a little baby.

Mary sang her praise. She magnified the Lord by telling what great things He was doing.

"He remembered me," she said. "He has done great things for me. He's showing his mercy to everyone. He does mighty deeds!"

In Psalm 34, David says, "O come magnify the LORD with me." God is infinite, so you can't make him greater than he already is. What does David mean? He means that you should *see* God as he really is. You should focus your attention on him. You can talk about him, so that your friends see things about him they have never seen before.

It's a little like looking at bacteria in a microscope. Bacteria are the smallest organisms that can be seen with a microscope. They're so small it takes ten thousand of them placed end to end to equal one centimeter. And yet, thousands of bacteria live in a tiny drop of water.

Through the microscope's lenses, bacteria appear forty, a hundred, or four hundred times larger than they actually are. When you turn the knob to focus the slide clearly, you can see bacteria with little tails, called flagella, they use to swim around. You can see the hairs, called fili, bacteria use to attach to other cells. You can see the wall around their bodies that is

a bit like skin. It all looks so big through the lenses. The bacteria don't actually get bigger when you look at them under the microscope; they just seem bigger and clearer. They're magnified.

Read the rest of Psalm 34, and you'll see what David did to magnify the LORD. He talked about all the things God had done for him. He focused on how great God is. God answered his prayers. God helped him when he was in trouble. God sent angels to watch over him. God gave him the things he needed. God stayed close to him when he was sad. God kept his body safe from harm. God is good!

Praise Project

Gadal means to magnify the Lord. Our word magnificent comes from the same root word. God is magnificent. Focus your attention on him. Look for ways to see his work throughout your day. Praise him.

When you wake up in the morning, praise him for making the earth turn on its axis. When you see the sun shining, praise him for the way he cares for the flowers and plants. When you have breakfast, praise him for giving you food. Praise him for your family. Praise him for your friends. Praise him for helping you learn at school. Praise him for being so magnificent. Magnify him!

Towdah:

TO BE THANKFUL

I will offer to you the sacrifice of thanksgiving, and will call upon the name of the LORD (Psalm 116:17 NKJV).

The tradition in Jesus' day was to greet a guest with a kiss on the cheek. It was like greeting someone today with a handshake or a hug. It meant that the person was welcome in your house. Tradition also called for a bowl of water to be brought to the guest. The roads in Jerusalem were hot and dusty. When a traveler came for a visit, even if it wasn't from very far away, he needed to wash the dust off his feet to feel refreshed and clean.

One day Jesus came to a small village. Among the people who lived in the village was a woman no one would talk to. She wasn't a good woman. She had done bad things, and everyone in the village knew about them. The woman heard the villagers talking. They were excited about something, so she listened.

Simon, who was one of the Pharisees, had invited Jesus to come for dinner. Jesus was at Simon's house.

The woman hurried home. She pulled an expensive bottle of perfume from the place it was hidden. She tucked it under her arm and rushed to Simon's house. She didn't knock or wait to be invited. She just rushed in and fell down at Jesus' feet. She knelt there at his feet and cried.

Her tears dropped onto Jesus' dirty feet. She let her hair fall down and she used it to wipe his feet and dry them. Then she kissed them. She was very tender, very gentle. When she was done, she opened the perfume and poured it over his feet.

Simon was shocked. "If Jesus were really a prophet, he would know what kind of woman was touching him," he thought.

Jesus looked up at Simon. "I have something to tell you, Simon" he said. "Two men owed money to a banker. Neither one could pay his bill, so the banker cancelled their debts. Which of the two would be more grateful?"

"Well," Simon said, "I suppose it would be the one who was forgiven the most."

"That's right," Jesus said. Then he turned to the woman, but he was still speaking to Simon. "Do you see this woman? I came to your house, but you brought no water for me to wash my feet. She has rained tears on my feet and dried them with her hair. You didn't greet me, but she hasn't stopped kissing my feet. You did nothing to refresh me, but she has soothed my feet with perfume. She was forgiven many sins. So she is very grateful."

Then he said to the woman, "Your sins are forgiven. Go in peace."

Have you ever done something that you weren't very proud of? Something that you knew you shouldn't have done? Jesus is willing to forgive every single sin if you will tell him what you've done.

When you do things you know are wrong, you feel all out of sorts with yourself. You might get irritable with your friends or your family. You feel like God has moved far away from you. But when you confess your sin and ask him to forgive you, he does. And you discover that you are at peace again.

Just as Jesus forgave the woman all her sins, he forgives yours too. Then the best thing you can do is to say "thank you." You don't have Jesus here physically to bow down at his feet like the woman in the story, but you can bow down with your praise. This kind of praise is called the sacrifice of thanksgiving.

A sacrifice means you offer something to God. In the Old Testament, the thank offering was one of the sacrifices the people brought to the altar. It was a way to say thank you to God for forgiving their sin. It was also called a peace offering because that person was finally at peace with God and with himself.

The word for this kind of praise is *towdah*. It's praise that results from being thankful. The word comes from the same word we studied earlier, *yadah*. This time the hand is extended in thanksgiving.

Praise Project

Do you feel peaceful knowing that God has forgiven you for the wrong things you have done? If you don't, then talk to God about it. Kneel down before him, reach out your hands, as though you were giving him your sacrifice of thanksgiving. Call out to him. Say thank you, thank you, thank you. That's *towdah*. Thank you, Lord.

Tehillah:

TO SING A NEW SONG

He put a new song in my mouth, a hymn of praise to our God. Many will see and fear and put their trust in the LORD (Psalm 40:3).

"Set my people free!"

Moses had said it again and again to Pharaoh. The Israelites, thousands of men, women and children were slaves in Egypt. God wanted his people free, so he sent Moses.

"Set my people free!" Moses said.

Each time Pharaoh said "No," God sent a plague. The rivers turned to blood. There were frogs, then gnats, then flies. The livestock died. There were boils, then hail, then locusts. Darkness covered the land. Then worst of all, every first-born son in Egypt died.

Pharaoh had enough. "Go!" he finally said.

The Israelites were ready. They grabbed their belongings and rushed out of Egypt. God led them with a Pillar of Cloud in the day. At night, a Pillar of Fire was their guide. They followed the Pillar of Cloud and Fire into the desert near the

Red Sea.

When Pharaoh heard that the Israelites had really gone, he changed his mind. Trouble was coming. He harnessed his chariots and gathered his army and raced after them. The Israelites looked up and saw the Egyptian army coming. They were terrified.

"Did you bring us out here in the desert to die?" they said to Moses. "We were better off in Egypt."

"Don't be afraid," Moses told them. "Just watch, and you'll see how God saves you."

The cloud moved from the front to the rear of the people. It stayed between the Israelites and the Egyptians. It gave light to the Israelites, but kept the Egyptians in the dark.

Moses stretched out his hand over the sea, and God sent a terrific wind that split the sea apart. The Israelites walked through on dry ground. Walls of water stood high on each side of them.

The Egyptians came fast. They raced into the middle of the sea. By now it was almost morning. God looked down from the Pillar of Cloud and Fire. He made their chariot wheels stick in the mud. The Egyptians panicked.

"Run," they shouted. "God is fighting on their side!"

God told Moses to stretch out his hand over the sea again. The walls of water crashed down on the Egyptians and drowned them all. The Israelites were safe.

The people were in awe of God's mighty power. Right there on the banks of the Red Sea, Moses and the Israelites sang a song about what God had done. The women picked up tambourines and danced to the song. This is what they sang:

I'm singing my heart out to God—what a victory!

He pitched horse and rider into the sea.

God is my strength, God is my song,

And yes! God is my salvation.

This is the kind of God I have

And I'm telling the world!

This is the God of my father—

I'm spreading the news far and wide!

God is a fighter,

Pure God, through and through.

Pharaoh's chariots and army

He dumped in the sea.

(from The Message Exodus 15:1-4)

Imagine how frightened the Israelites must have been. A whole army chasing after them and nowhere to go except the sea. No one had ever seen the sea split open before. They were completely unprepared for the way God delivered them. They must have stood on the shore and stared at the sea. It had just swallowed an entire army.

Then maybe someone took a deep breath and said, "Wow!" Someone else probably laughed with relief. Can you imagine the children clapping their hands and jumping up and down? Everyone started to rejoice, and suddenly Moses belted out a song. Not a song he knew. Not one he sang in Egypt or in the desert. He sang a brand new song. A song that no one had ever heard before. A song he made up on the spot to celebrate what had just happened.

That's what Psalm 40:3 means when it says, "He put a new song in my mouth, a hymn of praise to our God." The Hebrews called it a *tehillah*, a new song that tells about the mighty things God has done.

Praise Project
Read the rest of Moses' song in Exodus 15. Think of something that God has done that makes you remember how wonderful he is. Maybe he kept you safe in a dangerous place or helped you get well when you were sick. Have you seen a sunrise or a rainbow and thought about how great God is? Then you can sing a new song. Make up the words and the tune as you go along. If that seems hard to you, then choose a melody you know and put new words to it. Sing a song about how great God is, about how much he loves you, about how he takes care of you. Sing. *Tehillah!*

Zamar:

TO SING AND MAKE MUSIC WITH INSTRUMENTS

Give thanks to the L*ORD* *with the lyre; sing praises to him with a harp of ten strings (Psalm 33:2* NASB*).*

After King David died, his son Solomon became king. Solomon was a young man, probably between fifteen and twenty years old. The new king went to the tabernacle to worship God. While he was there, God came to him in a dream and said, "What do you want me to give you? Just ask me."

Solomon answered him. "You loved my father, David, and were kind to him. He lived faithfully in your presence, his relationships were just, and his heart was right. And you've continued to show your love to him by giving him a son to sit on his throne and be king after him. And now here I am. You're my God. You have made me, your servant, ruler over this kingdom. I'm too young for this. I don't know how to rule these people you have chosen, a great people, too many to even count.

"This is what I want," Solomon continued. "Give me a heart that listens to you, so I can lead your people well. Let me discern the difference between good and evil, for who on their own could lead your people?"

God was pleased with Solomon's answer. "Since you have asked for this," he said to Solomon, "and you haven't asked for long life or riches or the doom of your enemies, I will give you what you asked. I'm giving you a wise and mature heart. There has never been one so wise before you, nor will anyone come after you with as much wisdom. And I'm giving you the wealth and glory you didn't ask for too. If you walk in my ways and follow my commands, like David your father did, then I will give you a long life."

What a dream! When Solomon woke up, he returned to Jerusalem. He took his place as king. He worshipped before the Ark of the Covenant. Then he held a dinner celebration for everyone in his service.

King Solomon was a wise man. There was nothing he didn't understand. He knew all about plants, from the giant cedars of Lebanon to the tiny hyssop flower that grew in the cracks of the walls around Jerusalem. He knew everything about animals and birds, reptiles and fish. People came from all over to hear him talk. He always knew what decision to make when people came to him to solve a quarrel.

Solomon had been king for only four years when he decided to build a house for God. The temple would be a place for the Ark of the Covenant. It was always kept in the tabernacle, a kind of tent constructed by Moses. Now Solomon would build a temple, a building of wood and stone, but it would be a big job.

Solomon sent workers to Lebanon to help cut the cedars for wood. Thirty thousand workers. He sent them in shifts—ten thousand each month. They worked a month in Lebanon, then came home for two months. Solomon had another seventy thousand workers that did odd jobs. He had eighty thousand stonecutters in the hills of Israel. They quarried huge blocks of the best stone for the foundation.

It took seven long years to finish building the temple. When the work was finally done, Solomon called in all the leaders of Israel to help bring up the Ark of the Covenant. This chest was the most important thing placed in the temple. It held the stone tablets God gave to Moses as a sign of the covenant with his people. When all the leaders were ready, the priests carried the ark with long poles. They took it into the temple, to the inner room called the Holy of Holies.

All the musicians were ready, dressed in their robes. Four thousand musicians waited to praise God. There were stringed instruments, like the harp and

the lyre. There were wind instruments, like the flute and the pipes. There were horns—the shofar made from a ram's horn and trumpets made from brass. The tambourine, the cymbals, and the sistra (a type of rattle or shaker) were the percussion instruments. Solomon had an entire orchestra worshipping God. The musicians praised God together with the singers.

"God is good; his love goes on forever," they sang.

God was pleased with the temple. He was pleased with Solomon. He was pleased with the people praising him. A cloud came and filled the temple. It was the same cloud that led the Israelites through the Red Sea. It was the presence of God. The glory of God filled the temple.

Solomon prayed. "God, there is no God like you in the skies above or the earth below who keeps his covenant with his people and loves them like you. You did exactly what you promised. Is it possible, O God, that you have come to live in this place? The whole earth isn't big enough for you, let alone this temple I have built. But I'm asking you to come. Listen from heaven and forgive our sins."

Solomon praised God. The people of Israel praised with their songs. The musicians praised with their instruments. And God's glory came and filled the temple. Praise brings God's presence to his people. Praise him and his presence will surround you too.

Praise Project

If you play an instrument, pull it out and play a melody for God. Make something up as you go along. Play any notes that you want, but play them to the Lord. Just like you would sing a song to him. Your song might be fast and happy. It might be slow and worshipful. God is in the room with you. He's listening.

If you don't play an instrument, then experiment with the rhythm of a song. Make a tambourine with a paper plate or play a drum beat on a box or table top. Find a bell and ring it as you sing. His presence will come. You'll feel it.

Sing and make music to the Lord. That's what *zamar* means.

Ruwa:

TO SHOUT

God is gone up with a shout, the LORD *with the sound of a trumpet (Psalm 47:5* KJV*).*

It was almost noon in Jerusalem, but people still stood on the hill outside the city. The sun had been bright all morning, but now the sky turned an eerie dark. Roman guards played dice beneath the three men hanging on crosses. They paid no attention to Jesus in the center or the two thieves on either side. Suddenly there was an earthquake. Rocks split into pieces. The soldiers picked up their spears and rushed to their posts. Frightened people ran for cover.

Only a few stayed near the cross. Jesus' mother, with some of the women who had served Jesus. John, his beloved disciple. In his final words, Jesus had given his mother into John's care.

Jesus was dead.

When the earth stopped trembling, the soldiers took the bodies of the dead men off the crosses. Jesus' friends took him away from the hill, called the Place of the Skull, and buried him in a borrowed tomb.

What now? The disciples had left their homes and

families and followed him around for three years. The women had watched his miracles and cared for his needs. Now he was gone. There was nothing they could do. The disciples went fishing. The women grieved.

Three days later the most amazing miracle of all happened. Jesus rose from the dead!

It was almost impossible to believe, but it was true. He appeared to the women. He appeared to the disciples in their meeting place. The doors were closed, but suddenly Jesus was there with them. He talked with them and ate with them. He showed them the scars on his hands and feet and the wound in his side. He taught them for forty days. Then one day he took them to a place outside the city. He raised his hands and blessed them. And while he was blessing them, he disappeared into the clouds and was gone.

The disciples stood staring into an empty sky. They were astonished.

Two angels appeared and said, "Why are you standing here? This same Jesus who was taken into heaven will come back the same way you saw him go."

The disciples fell to their knees and worshipped. They returned to Jerusalem bursting with joy and praising God. What an amazing story they had to tell! That's what happened here on earth. But have you ever wondered what happened in heaven? From the very beginning of time, God knew men would choose their own way. God knew they would need a savior to come to earth and show them what God was really like. He knew they would need someone to pay the price for their sin. Jesus was willing to leave his throne in heaven and accomplish the task. He came to earth, lived a sinless life, and told people about God. He died on a cross as the sacrifice for the sins of all humanity. Then he went back to heaven. And all of heaven rejoiced to see their king return to his throne.

Long before it actually happened, David wrote about what it would be like. You can read this in Psalms 24 and 47.

The angels stand at the gates of heaven to welcome the returning king. They shout back and forth to each other, "Lift up your heads, O you gates; be lifted up, you ancient doors that the King of glory may come in."

A chorus of angels returns the shout. "Who is this King of glory?" Another band of angels answers. "The LORD strong and mighty, the LORD mighty in battle. He is the King of glory."

Jesus marches through the gates of heaven to the shouts of angels and the blare of trumpets. "God has gone up with a shout, the LORD with the sounding of trumpets! For God is King of all the earth. He is seated on his holy throne!" He returns to his throne at the right hand of God, the Father.

All the angels in heaven are waiting for the Son of God to return. They shout for joy as he sits down at the right hand of his Father. It's a victory shout! He has done it. He triumphed over sin, over Satan, over death itself. He has won. He rules. He sits on the throne. He is the King over all the earth.

If you're a sports fan, you know what it means to shout for your team at a game. Maybe you have shouted with excitement when your favorite player scored a goal. That's what *ruwa* means. To shout in triumph or joy. It can be a battle cry that says, "Yes! Go! Win!" You can shout to God with the same energy that you use at the ball game.

You can shout like the angels in heaven. Rejoice that God has given you victory over your sin – over selfishness, pride, envy, anger, hatred. He's given you victory over the devil – the accusations, guilt, and lies he tries to make you believe. He's given you a place in the family of God – the freedom to come boldly into God's presence and call him Abba, Daddy.

Praise Project

Find a place that you can shout to the Lord. You might have to go outside somewhere. Remember, God loves you. He sent Jesus to die for you. Jesus has gone to heaven, and he's going to take you there one day, too. That's something to shout about. Shout for joy!

Shabach:

TO COMMEND

One generation shall praise thy works to another, and shall declare thy mighty acts (Psalm 145:4 KJV).

The word *commend* means to say something is worthy of your trust. It's an endorsement. Sports figures often make endorsements. They tell you to buy these tennis shoes because they're the best or eat this breakfast cereal because it will make you strong. When was the last time you told your friends about a good book or a new song or something else you really liked?

"Billy, you've got to see this movie. It was so funny I spilled popcorn all over myself!"

"Candace, can you come over after school? I've got to show you my new phone. It's loaded. It's got everything."

That's what it means to commend something. You want to tell someone about your experience. You want to recommend they check it out too.

In the days when Elisha was God's prophet to Israel, there was a little girl—we'll call her Mara, though the Bible doesn't name her. Mara was stolen from her family and carried off to be a slave in Syria. Even though Israel and Syria weren't at war with each other, men from both sides destroyed villages on the border and carried people away to be sold as slaves. Mara was given to Naaman, as a servant for his wife.

Naaman was the commander of the army of Syria. He was a brave soldier, well-loved by his king. He had won many battles, but Naaman was sick. He had a skin disease, and there was no cure for it. Eventually the disease would take his life.

One day, Mara was caring for her mistress. Maybe she was straightening the fine silk curtains that hung around the woman's bed. Maybe she was combing the woman's hair. Naaman's wife was sad about her husband's disease. She probably talked to Mara about how worried she was. Even though she was a slave, Mara's heart ached for her master and his wife. She wanted to help, so she told her mistress about the prophet in her homeland. "If only my master could meet the prophet of Israel, he would be healed of his skin disease."

When Naaman heard what Mara had said, he went immediately to the king and told him about this prophet. The king of Syria wrote a letter to the king of Israel and sent Naaman to him. The letter said, "When you receive this letter, you'll know that I have personally sent my servant Naaman to you. Heal him of his skin disease." Naaman traveled to Samaria, where the king of Israel lived and presented his letter.

The king of Israel read the letter. He was so upset, he tore his robes. "Does he think I'm a god with the power of life and death? He sends me orders to heal this man! What's going on? He's trying to pick a fight with me. That's it."

Elisha the prophet of God heard what had happened. He sent a message to the king of Israel. "Why are you so upset? Send him to me and he'll learn there's a God and his prophet in Israel." So the king sent Naaman to see Elisha.

Naaman and his horses and chariots rode up to the door of Elisha's simple house. Elisha didn't even bother to go to the door. He sent a servant out to give Naaman a message. "Go to the River Jordan and plunge yourself into it seven times. Your skin will be healed."

Naaman was infuriated. "I thought he would personally come out and meet me. I thought he would call on the name of God, wave his hand over the diseased spot, and heal it. The rivers of Syria are cleaner by far than any river in Israel. Why not bathe in them? At least I'd be clean when I finished." Naaman stomped off.

But his servants ran after him. "Sir," they said, "if the prophet had asked you to do something hard and heroic, wouldn't you have done it? So why not do this simple thing?"

Naaman listened to them. He went down to the Jordan and washed himself. Again and again he let his body sink down into the muddy waters. Four. Five. Six times he sank and rose from the water. When he rose the seventh time, his skin was healed. It was as pink as a new-born baby's skin. He was as good as new.

Naaman rushed back to Elisha. "I know beyond a shadow of a doubt that there is no God anywhere on earth other than the God of Israel. Let me give you a gift of thanks."

Elisha refused. He would not take Naaman's gift.

"If you won't take anything, then let me ask you for something. Give me a load of dirt from Israel, so that

I can build an altar to God. I'm never again going to worship any god other than God."

Elisha gave him the dirt, and Naaman set off toward home rejoicing.

Mara was only a little girl, and a slave in a strange country, but she knew her God. She commended God and his prophet to her mistress. Mara didn't know what would happen. She didn't know if Naaman would listen to her recommendation. She didn't know if he would go. Naaman's response was not in her control. The only thing she could do was commend her God. And that's what she did. As a result, Naaman was healed.

David commended God too. He commended God to his children, to his soldiers, to the priests at the temple, to all the people in his kingdom. He sang a song that commended God. He sang it so often he knew it by heart. He didn't have to think about what he wanted to sing or to say. It's called "David's Psalm of Praise."

"God is magnificent! There are no boundaries to his greatness. Generation after generation stands in awe of your work; each one tells stories of your mighty acts. God's beauty and splendor have everyone talking! Your marvelous works are headline news. I could write a book about how great you are. You're famous all over the country. God is always full of mercy and grace. He's not quick to be angry. He's rich in love. God is good to everyone!

"Creation and all its creatures clap for you. They talk about the glories of your rule. They let the world know about your power for good. Your kingdom is eternal. You never get voted out of office. God always does what he says. He gives a hand to those down on their luck. He gives a fresh start to those ready to quit. Everything God does is right. He's there listening to everyone who prays. He does what's best for those who fear him—he hears them call out and saves them. God sticks by all who love him.

"My mouth is filled with God's praise. Let everything living bless him, Bless his holy name from now to eternity!" (from *The Message* Psalm 145).

Praise Project

Make your own list of things that you could tell someone about God. How would you commend him to your friends or your parents or your brothers and sisters? Make your list into a psalm and memorize it. Use David's psalm of praise to help you. Sing it to God every morning and every night. Then ask God to give you someone to share it with. Commend him. Recommend him. That's *shabach*.

Barak:

TO BLESS

Thus will I bless thee while I live: I will lift up my hands in thy name (Psalm 63:4 KJV).

King David was having a bad day. It was worse than bad. Absalom had declared himself king. Absalom and David didn't get along very well. In fact, they hadn't spoken to each other in years. Absalom was so angry, he decided he would try to take over David's kingdom. If that wasn't enough, a messenger brought more bad news. The whole country had turned against David. They wanted Absalom to be king, instead of David.

"Let's get going!" David said. "We've got to get out of here before Absalom comes and kills us all!"

King David, his family and his servants packed up what they could carry and left the city. David's army marched out too. They passed through the city heading for safety. They crossed the Kidron, a small stream, and took the road that led to the wilderness.

David was so sad, he sent the priests back to Jerusalem with the Ark of the Covenant. The Ark was the symbol of God's presence. David wasn't sure if God still wanted him to be king. David and his followers climbed up the Mount of Olives.

When they started down the other side toward the Jordan Valley, one of David's old enemies came along beside them. His name was Shimei. He was one of King Saul's men before David became king. Shimei threw rocks at David. He shouted at David and called him names. "Get out of here," he said. "God is paying you back for what you did to Saul. Look at you — you're ruined! And stay out, you pitiful old man!"

One of David's men got angry. "Let me at him. I'll cut off his head!"

"No," David said, sadly. "Don't do that."

They went on. Shimei followed on the hill above them. He kept shouting and throwing stones and kicking dirt at them. By the time they reached the Jordan River, they were all exhausted.

Day after day, they marched on. Friends brought them food. They found places in the wilderness to rest. Somewhere along the way, David sang a song to the LORD. You can read it in Psalm 42.

He was discouraged. He was sad. He felt betrayed by his own son. But he sang anyway. He chose to look to God and to praise Him. He knew, even though everything around him looked really bad, God was still in control. God was still good. God still cared for him.

He sang, "God, you're my God. I'm in a wilderness, but I've seen your power. I know how much you love me, and that love is better than life. I will bless you. I will praise you as long as I live. I will lift up my hands in your name."

The Bible says all human beings have a body, a soul, and a spirit. Your body is the physical part of you – your muscles and bones, your heart and lungs, your senses that let you taste, hear, see, feel and smell. Your soul is your mind that lets you think, your will that lets you choose and your emotions that let you feel happy, sad, excited or disappointed. Your spirit is the part of you that senses God's presence and hears his voice. It's the place where God's spirit lives in you.

David knew it was important not to let his body and his soul decide how he would act. His body was tired. If Shimei's aim was good, David had bruises that probably hurt. He was sad and worried. But David talked to his soul. Here's what he said:

> *Why are you down in the dumps, dear soul?*
> *Why are you crying the blues?*
> *Fix my eyes on God—*
> *Soon I'll be praising again.*
> *He puts a smile on my face.*
> *He's my God.*
>
> (from **The Message** Psalm 42)

Praise Project

Everyone has bad days. Sometimes you just don't feel like praising God. You may feel sad or lonely. You may feel angry. Maybe something happened that seemed unfair. Sometimes you're tired or hungry or hurting physically, and you don't feel like praising God. The next time you have a bad day, do what David did. Remember that God is good. Remember how much he loves you.

Talk to your soul and say, "Bless the Lord anyway!"

Raqad:

TO DANCE, SKIP AND LEAP

Let them praise his name with dancing and make music to him with tambourine and harp (Psalm 149:3).

In the Bible, dancing is a form of celebration. Both men and women danced. Sometimes dancers moved in a circle or marched in a procession. Women danced when their soldiers were victorious. Miriam led a company of dancers after Pharaoh's army was swallowed by the water. Biblical dancers whirled, leaped, sprang, stamped their feet, jumped and skipped—always to express their joy for God's love, his presence, and his victory over the enemy. Even David, the king danced as he marched with the priests before the Ark of the Covenant.

From the days of Moses, the ark had been with the Israelites. It was the symbol of God's covenant with his people. It was a visible sign of his presence with them. The whole time they were in the wilderness, the priests marched with the ark. The ark went before them when they crossed through the Red Sea. Priests carried the ark into battle, as the Israelites fought in the Promised Land. In peaceful times, the ark stayed in the tabernacle at Shiloh.

One day, while Eli was the judge, the men of Israel went out to fight against the Philistines. The Philistines were winning. The men of Israel sent for the ark. They thought if the ark was with them, they couldn't possibly lose the battle. They cheered when the priests carried it into the camp.

The Philistines heard the shout, and they were afraid. They had heard stories of the ark. They knew it meant God's presence was with the army of Israel. This was the god who had struck the Egyptians with plagues. "Be strong, Philistines," they shouted to each other, "or you will be slaves of the Hebrews." So they fought hard against the Israelites, and they won. Many men of Israel were killed, and the Philistines captured the ark.

The ark had always blessed God's people, but it did just the opposite in the towns of the Philistines. They took the ark from city to city, but everywhere they left it, the people got sick. No one wanted the ark nearby. Finally the Philistines decided to give it back to Israel. They took it to a place near the town of Kiriath Jearim and sent a message to the Israelites to come and get it. So the Israelites came. They took the ark to the house of Abinadab, where his son, Eleazar, took care of it. And that's where it stayed for twenty years.

Soon Saul became king of Israel, but he never paid much attention to the ark. Saul never really understood the importance of God's presence. The ark remained

where it was and God's presence blessed Abinadab and his family.

When David became king after Saul, he wanted to bring the ark back to Jerusalem. He understood how important it was to have the ark to remind the people of God's presence with them. He wanted the people to be excited about God's presence. It had been a long time since anyone tried to move the ark. Even David had forgotten God's instructions about how it should be carried.

David went down to get the ark. They put it on a cart pulled by oxen. When it started to fall, a man named Uzzah put out his hand to steady the ark. As soon as he touched it, he fell down dead. No one was ever to touch the ark of God. David was upset and afraid. He didn't know how to get the ark back to Jerusalem. So he left it nearby at Obed-edom's house. It stayed there for months.

When David heard God was blessing Obed-edom, he decided he would try again. This time he followed all the laws for carrying the ark. The Levites, or priests, carried it on their shoulders with long poles. David took off his king's robe and wore a light-weight white robe like the other priests for the procession. When they came up the hill into Jerusalem, David danced with all his might! He leaped and whirled. He jumped and skipped. He was so happy to have God's presence with him and with his people.

It was a grand parade. The singers sang praise to God. The musicians blew their trumpets and crashed their cymbals. The people shouted praise. David danced and leaped for joy!

Praise Project

Play or sing your favorite praise songs. Maybe you like the fast praise songs, and you want to jump and skip and leap. Or maybe you like the slower praise songs and want to do things quietly and gracefully. Either way is fine. The important thing is to remember that you are praising God with your movements. The Bible even talks about God dancing joyfully over his people. Isn't that a wonderful picture?

Hannah's Prayer

My heart rejoices in the LORD *(1 Samuel 2:1).*

Hannah desperately wanted a son. Children were a sign of God's blessing, and Hannah had none. Her husband, Elkanah, had two wives, as many men did

at the time. Elkanah loved Hannah best and was very good to her. Penninah was the other wife. She had both sons and daughters.

Penninah was jealous of Hannah, so she teased her about having no children. She probably called her names and told her she was worthless. Hannah was so sad, she cried often. In fact, she was so upset by Penninah's bullying that she stopped eating.

Elkanah couldn't understand it. He begged Hannah to eat. He reassured her of his love, but still Hannah was sad. Every year Elkanah took his family and went up to Shiloh to worship the LORD at the tabernacle. One evening Hannah slipped away and went to the tabernacle to pray. She cried and prayed to the LORD. She said, "LORD, if you will just give me a son, then I will give him to the LORD all the days of his life." She stayed a long time and kept praying silently.

Eli, the high priest, saw Hannah's lips move, but could hear no words. He thought she had been drinking. "Woman," he said to her, "how long will you keep drinking? You need to stop."

Hannah lifted her head from her prayers and looked at him. "Oh, no, sir," she said. "I haven't been drinking. I am just so unhappy. I'm pouring my heart out to God, because I need his help."

Eli didn't ask why she was unhappy or what she wanted. "Go in peace," he said. "May God give you what you have asked."

And God did. God did love Hannah and he had a special plan for her. Israel needed a strong leader, one who would love God with all his heart and stand firm when the people of Israel needed guidance. God wanted Hannah to put all her longing, all her love into raising this special child.

Hannah had a son before the year was out. She named him Samuel. She stayed home with him for the first few years. She cared for him and taught him to love God with all his heart. Then, she took him to Shiloh.

Hannah found Eli, the priest. "I'm the woman who was praying to God," she said. "I prayed for this child, and God gave me what I wanted. Now I want to dedicate him to the LORD." Hannah left Samuel with Eli. He grew up in the temple and served God. She came to visit every year and brought Samuel a new linen coat like the priests wore. God had answered her prayer, and Hannah dedicated him to the LORD. Samuel became one of the greatest leaders Israel ever had.

Hannah had three more sons and two daughters, but none was as special as Samuel, the one she gave to the LORD.

Hannah succumbed to the bullying and pressure from Penninah. She believed the lies that made her feel worthless and discouraged. All the time, God was working in her heart. He knew she would be the perfect mother for Samuel. When she finally poured her heart out to God, Samuel was born. Hannah treasured him. She recognized God's gift. And she kept her promise to give him back to God. Hannah worshipped. She praised God for answering her prayers. This is her song:

> "My heart rejoices in the LORD;
> in the LORD my horn is lifted high.
> My mouth boasts over my enemies,
> for I delight in your deliverance.
> There is no one holy like the LORD;
> there is no one besides you;
> there is no Rock like our God."
>
> (1 Samuel 2:1-2)

Prayer Project

Hannah prayed silently to God when her heart was sad. After God answered her prayer, she prayed her thanks aloud. God hears the prayers you speak and the prayers you pray in your heart.

Is something in your life making you sad like Hannah? You have a High Priest, just as Hannah did. Jesus is your

High Priest who listens to the cries of your heart. Tell him what you need. Are there struggles in your family? Are you concerned about something at school? Have you lost a friendship? Pour your heart out to God, just as Hannah did in the temple. He will hear your words and meet the needs of your heart. Sing Hannah's song of praise. It can be your song too.

Jumpin' Jehoshaphat!

In God, whose word I praise, in God I trust; I will not be afraid (Psalm 56:4).

Jehoshaphat was the king of Judah. He was a good king. He loved God.

The Moabites and the Ammonites and the Meunites lived across the Dead Sea. They were the enemies of Judah. They decided to gang up on Jehoshaphat.

One day, the lookouts for the city rushed in to the king. "A huge army is on its way to fight you," they said. "They're already at the oasis of En Gedi. There's no time to waste!"

Jehoshaphat was afraid, so he prayed. He sent word throughout the land for all the people to pray too. He stood at the courtyard of the temple and prayed, "O LORD, you're the God who's in heaven. You rule over all the kingdoms. You're powerful and mighty, and no one can stand against you. God, we don't have the power to face this huge army. We don't know what to do."

All the men and women and children of Judah stood before the temple where Jehoshaphat prayed. They all prayed and waited to hear what God would say.

Then the Spirit of God spoke to Jahaziel, one of the priests, and told him to say this: "Listen. This is what the LORD says to you: Don't be afraid because of this army. The battle is not yours. It's God's. Tomorrow, march down there. You won't have to fight. Just stand still and watch God save you. Don't be discouraged, for God is with you."

Jehoshaphat was so glad to hear God's word that he bowed down with his face to the ground and worshipped. The priests stood up and began to praise God. They shouted praise at the top of their lungs.

The next morning everyone was up early. Jehoshaphat gathered all the people and said, "Believe God! Believe God and you will be safe."

The people were ready to march, but first Jehoshaphat appointed singers for a choir. He told them to sing

praises to the LORD. Then he put them at the front of the army to lead the way. They went out singing, "Give thanks to the LORD, for his love never fails!"

As they sang, God set ambushes against their enemies. He confused the enemy soldiers. The Ammonites and the Moabites thought they were attacking the men of Judah. Instead, they killed the Meunites. Then the Moabites started fighting the Ammonites. They fought each other until all the enemy army was dead.

When Jehoshaphat and his army came over the hill, there was no one left to fight. They were amazed at what God did. God won the battle, just as he said he would. The people of Judah blessed God, right there on the battlefield. After that the place was called the Valley of Blessing. Jehoshaphat led them back to

Jerusalem. It was a celebration parade. They went to the Temple worshipping God with harps and lutes and trumpets and songs.

Do you think the people of Judah were scared? Do you think the singers were praising God with their knees shaking? Maybe so. It would have been easy to be scared and forget what God said to them. If they had tried to fight the battle on their own, they might have been destroyed. But they didn't. They believed God. They praised him, and God worked a miracle.

It's not easy to praise God when things look bad. It takes faith. God loves that kind of faith. He loves it when you believe what he says. He loves it when you trust him to take care of you.

Praise Project

Are you afraid of something? Do what Jehoshaphat did. Talk to God about it. Read Jehoshaphat's prayer in 2 Chronicles 20:6-12. Start your prayer by praising God for his great power. Remind him of all the great things he has done. Then, tell him about your problem. Ask him to speak to you and listen for his answer. You may hear him speak in your heart. Sometimes his answer may come through another person. Be obedient to his word. Praise him as you face your battle and watch as he rescues you and leads you to victory.

A Den of Lions

Now when Daniel learned that the decree had been published, he went home to his upstairs room where the windows opened towards Jerusalem. Three times a day he got down on his knees and prayed, giving thanks to his God, just as he had done before (Daniel 6:10).

Daniel was a young man when the Babylonian King Nebuchadnezzar declared war on Jerusalem and took slaves to Babylon. Nebuchadnezzar wanted young men of Israel who were healthy and handsome. He wanted well-educated boys who could be trained in the Babylonian language and learn magic and fortune-telling.

Daniel was smart, both in his studies and in the decisions he made in everyday life. He learned the customs of Babylon, the language, and how the government worked. At the end of his training, the king chose Daniel to serve him.

Daniel served well. God had given him the special gift of understanding dreams. He interpreted dreams for the king. Whenever the king consulted him about anything, Daniel's answers were always better than the answers the Babylonian magicians gave. So Daniel rose to higher and higher positions. The Babylonian magicians were jealous.

When Nebuchadnezzar died, Daniel served his son, King Belshazzar. When Belshazzar died, Daniel served the new King Darius.

Daniel always spoke truth to the kings he served. He always told them that God had given them their kingdoms. He told them that God would take their kingdoms away if they ignored him. Daniel prayed and worshipped God every day. Every morning, every day at noon, and every night, Daniel went to his room and asked God for wisdom. He prayed for his homeland, he prayed for his king, and he praised God.

King Darius was so impressed with Daniel's ability to rule wisely and well, he put Daniel in charge of the whole kingdom. The old governors were jealous. They began to look for ways to get rid of him, but Daniel was trustworthy. He did his job well. They couldn't find any reason to accuse him to King Darius.

"We'll never find anything wrong with him, unless we can trap him somehow," they said. "Unless we can come up with some religious reason to get him in trouble."

So they plotted together, then they went to the king.

"King Darius, live forever!" they said. "All of your rulers have gotten together and decided that you should make this decree." They read the decree to him.

"For the next thirty days no one is to pray to any god or man, except you.

Anyone who disobeys will be thrown into the lion's den."

King Darius thought it was a good idea. He liked the idea that everyone would pray to him, so he had the decree written out. He signed it and posted it throughout the kingdom.

When Daniel heard about the decree, he continued to pray just as he always did. He knelt before the open window of his room that faced Jerusalem and prayed for the home he loved. He thanked God and praised him.

The scheming governors came to Daniel's room and found him praying and asking God for help. They went straight to the King.

"Didn't you sign a decree forbidding anyone to pray to any god or man except you?"

"Yes, I did," the king answered.

"Well, Daniel ignores you, O king. He defies your decree and prays three times a day to his God."

The king was terribly upset, because he liked Daniel. He spent the day trying to find a way to save Daniel from the lion's den.

Before long the governors came back. "Remember, O king, it's the law that your decree cannot be changed."

The king knew it was true. There was nothing he could do, but command that Daniel be thrown in with the lions.

"Daniel," the king shouted into the pit, "may the God you serve rescue you!"

Then they placed a stone over the opening and sealed it.

The king went back to his palace. He couldn't eat. He couldn't sleep. He paced back and forth in his chambers. When the sun rose, he rushed to the lion's den.

"Daniel," he shouted after the stone was removed. "Daniel, servant of the living God, has your God saved you from the lions?"

76

"Live forever, O king," Daniel answered. "My God sent his angel and closed the mouths of the lions. They haven't hurt me. I am innocent before God and before you, O king. I have done nothing to harm you."

King Darius was delighted. He had Daniel taken out of the den. When the king looked at him, Daniel didn't have even a scratch on him. He had trusted God. The king had the wicked governors who plotted against Daniel thrown into the lions' den. Then he declared that Daniel's God should be worshipped all through his kingdom.

Daniel continued to be faithful to his king and to his God. He went back to his work. He went back to his routine. He prayed every morning, every noon, and every night.

Praise Project

Daniel may have praised God with the same words that King Darius used when he made his last decree. This is what Darius said about God:

"He is the living God, world without end.

His kingdom never fails.

He rules eternally.

He is a savior and a rescuer.

He performs astonishing miracles in heaven

and on earth.

He saved Daniel from the power of the lions."

(Daniel 6:26-27)

You can pray and praise like Daniel did. Take a few minutes in the morning to praise him. Stop at lunchtime and remember to praise him. At bedtime, praise him again. Use King Darius' words if you need help getting started. Then go on to add your own words of praise. Try this every day for a week and see what happens.

Startled Shepherds

The shepherds returned, glorifying and praising God for all the things they had heard and seen, which were just as they had been told (Luke 2:20).

The night sky was dark. It was quiet in the hills around Bethlehem. Sheep huddled together in little groups nibbling grass. From time to time, one dropped its head and slept. A few shepherds stood guard, watching for hungry lions or bears. The only sound was an occasional call of a mother ewe to her baby lamb.

Suddenly the quiet of the night was shattered. An angel stood among the sheep. The dark sky blazed with light. The terrified shepherds fell to the ground. What was happening? Were they all about to die?

The angel spoke. "Don't be afraid. I've come to bring you good news. Great joy for all people."

The shepherds trembled, but they listened, amazed.

"Today in Bethlehem a Savior is born to you. He is Christ the Lord. Look for a baby, wrapped in cloths, lying in a manger."

The whole sky was filled with angels. A huge choir of angels singing praises to God. "Glory to God in the highest!" they sang.

And then they were gone, back into heaven.

The shepherds looked at one another. "Let's go," they said. "Let's go see if it's true." So they ran toward the town of Bethlehem. They searched the stables until they found Mary and Joseph and the baby. They could hardly believe their eyes, but it was real. Just as the angel had told them. This little baby, surrounded by hay and barn animals, was something special.

Maybe one of the shepherds reached out a hand and touched the baby Jesus' cheek. As they looked into Mary's eyes, maybe they wondered if she knew what they knew. Maybe they told Mary and Joseph

what the angels had said. That this was the son of God and the Savior of the world. They knelt beside the manger, the place where the animals ate, and looked at a miracle lying in the hay. The Messiah, Emmanuel, God with us, God with you.

The excited shepherds tiptoed from the stable to return to their fields. They had seen angels. God had sent a Savior and he told them, just ordinary shepherds. They had seen the child. They couldn't stop talking. They told everyone they met as they left Bethlehem. They returned to their sheep praising God. They praised him for sending the angels to them. They

praised him for telling them about the baby, Jesus. They praised him for sending a savior. They praised him for letting them see the child. They praised!

The shepherds were just plain, simple people. They were poor. They lived outside with the animals. They weren't educated like the scribes or the priests. They weren't important or popular, but God chose them to deliver his message about the Messiah.

It's so easy to get caught in the popularity trap. The trap says you need the right clothes, the right shoes, the right house or job or college. But that's not what God says. God says you are important, valued, even beloved. You are important because you are his, because he made you. Jesus comes to you, just as he came to the stable and the shepherds, the ones who knew stables well. Whether you're rich or poor, pretty or plain, strong or simple, look into the manger. He came for you.

Praise Project

God showed the shepherds what he was doing. He let them in on his plans for the world. God will let you in on his plans too, if you ask him. Ask him to show you what he's doing in your family and friendships, what he's doing through your struggles. Listen to what he says. Then praise him with the song the angels sang, "Glory to God in the highest!"

A Lame Man Walks

He jumped to his feet and began to walk. Then he went with them into the temple courts, walking and jumping, and praising God (Acts 3:8).

A lame man begged beside the gate of the temple in Jerusalem. The Bible doesn't tell us the man's name, so in this story we'll call him Timon. Timon had been crippled since birth. Now, as a grown man, he had no way to earn a living. Every day Timon's friends carried him to the temple and sat him beside the Beautiful Gate. This gate was the main entrance to the temple. Whenever anyone came, Timon called out to them.

"Alms. Alms for the poor," he said.

People passed him going in to worship. They passed him when they left to go home. The dust from their sandals swirled around Timon's clothes. Sometimes it made him cough. Timon held out his hands whenever anyone passed, hoping they might give him a little money.

Peter and John, the two apostles, were going to the temple one afternoon to pray. Since Jesus ascended into heaven, they had prayed and preached and taught in the name of Jesus and in the power of the Holy Spirit. When they got to the Beautiful Gate, they saw Timon. They must have felt sadness when they looked at him. They must have heard the Holy Spirit within them saying to heal the man. They stopped and looked at him.

Maybe Timon had been ignored by so many people that day, he wasn't even looking at the two men who stopped in front of him.

"Look at us," Peter said.

Timon looked up. He thought they were going to give him money.

"I don't have any gold or silver," Peter said. "But what I do have, I'll give you."

Timon needed money to live. He had never considered needing anything else. What could these men possibly have to give him? Timon held up his

hands, willing to take whatever they had to offer, but Peter's hands were empty.

Looking him straight in the eye, Peter said, "In the name of Jesus Christ of Nazareth, walk."

Timon must have stared at them. Maybe he thought they were taunting him. Certainly he wanted to walk, but he had never taken a step in his life. Now here were two strangers commanding him to walk. Were they crazy?

Peter reached down and took Timon's right hand and helped him up. All of a sudden, Timon's feet and ankles became firm. He jumped to his feet and walked! He walked with Peter and John into the temple. He walked back and forth across the courtyard. He leaped up and down. He praised God for a gift better than money.

Praise Project

Can you think of something you need? Is it what you really need? Timon thought he needed more money. If someone had given him money, he would just be a crippled man with a little cash. What he really needed was healing, and that's what Peter and John gave him. That's what God gave him.

As you pray, ask God to give you what you really need. Watch and see what he does, and praise him for it.

Earthquake!

About midnight Paul and Silas were praying and singing hymns to God, and the other prisoners were listening to them. Suddenly there was such a violent earthquake that the foundations of the prison were shaken. At once all the prison doors flew open, and everybody's chains came loose (Acts 16:25-26).

Paul and Silas were on a journey to spread the news about Jesus and God's love. They stopped in Philippi, a Roman colony. One day when they were going to a place to pray, they ran into a slave girl who was a fortune teller. She made a lot of money for her masters by telling fortunes.

She followed Paul and Silas around, shouting. "These men are servants of the most high God. They are telling you the way to be saved."

Paul and Silas tried to ignore her. They knew that an evil spirit gave her the ability to tell fortunes. They were sad because the evil spirit had power over her.

The next day the same thing happened again. The woman followed them through the city shouting her message to anyone who would listen. Whenever Paul or Silas tried to talk to people gathered in the city, the woman shouted at them.

Finally, after days of her pestering shouts, Paul was upset. He wanted the evil spirit to leave him alone. He wanted it to leave the woman alone. So he turned around and spoke to the spirit.

"In the name of Jesus Christ," he said, "I command you to get out of her."

And the evil spirit left. Just like that.

When the girl's owners realized she couldn't tell fortunes anymore, they were angry. Their business would go bankrupt without her. They had Paul and Silas arrested, beaten up, and thrown into jail.

The jailer took them to an inner cell in the prison, fastened irons on their legs, and left them. It was damp and dark, and the air smelled sour. The welts on Paul's back throbbed. Silas rubbed the bruises on his arms and legs. They hurt, but they didn't get depressed or hopeless.

About midnight, Paul and Silas were praying and singing praises to God. The other prisoners couldn't believe their ears. These men had been beaten black and blue. They were in a maximum security cell in a Roman prison. And they were singing. What kind of people were they?

Then, without any warning, a violent earthquake shook the whole place. All the prison doors flew open. The chains fell off the prisoners. They were all loose.

Paul and Silas and the prisoners were so shocked by what happened, they didn't know what to do.

The noise startled the sleeping jailer. He panicked when he saw all the doors swinging open. He knew he would be blamed, so he picked up his sword to kill himself.

Paul shouted at him. "Don't do that. We're still here," he said. "Nobody has run away."

The jailer grabbed a torch and ran into the cell. When he saw Paul and Silas still there, he was astonished. He collapsed on the ground in front of them. "What must I do to be saved?" he asked.

"Believe in the Lord Jesus and you will be saved," Paul told him.

The jailer took them to his house and washed their wounds. He and his family were all baptized that night. Then they shared a meal together. It was a celebration in the middle of the night. The jailer was filled with joy because he believed in God.

Praise Project

It seemed impossible that Paul and Silas would get out of that jail cell, but God did a miracle and opened the prison doors. Are there things in your life that seem impossible to fix? Maybe you have a problem with a friend or your parents. Maybe you've had to transfer to a new school and finding new friends seems impossible. Maybe your dad or mom has lost a job and life seems harder than it ever has before. Sometimes circumstances like these can feel like a prison. Maybe your heart aches, just like Paul's back. Can you praise in the middle of it, the way Paul and Silas did? It may seem hard, but begin to praise. Find a song or a verse that you can sing to the Lord and praise him with it. Then watch God rescue you.

Because God is Awesome!

O Lord our Lord, how majestic is your name in all the earth!
(Psalm 8:1-2).

Have you ever thought about how big the universe is? Have you tried to count the stars on a clear night or wondered how far it is to Venus? Imagine you could strap a saddle onto a beam of light. Light is the fastest

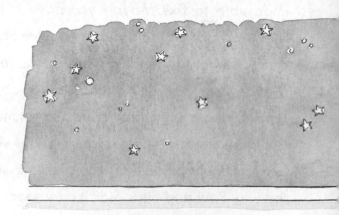

thing in the universe. It travels 186,000 miles every second. That's almost the distance from the earth to the moon.

If you started at the sun and rode your photo-charged flying machine, you would reach earth in about eight minutes. In five and a half hours, you would reach Pluto. From there, it would take over four years to reach Alpha Centauri A, our nearest star. In a hundred thousand years you would be able to see the entire spiral of the Milky Way, our galaxy. It would take fifty million years before you would see points of light that aren't stars, but galaxies. Thousands of galaxies, just like our Milky Way. In thirteen billion years, you would finally reach the edge of the visible universe. That's big! Or maybe *awesome* is a better word.

David might have been sitting under the stars when he wrote Psalm 8. Maybe he was wondering how far away they were, too. He felt small in comparison to the vast universe. In verse three, he says, "When I consider your heavens, the work of your fingers, the moon and the stars, which you have set in place, what is man that you are mindful of him, the son of man that you care for him?" When David considered the stars, he could only ask "Who am I?"

David answered his own question. He realized that God thinks we're pretty important. When he says *man*, he means *mankind*. Not just a man or a woman or a boy or girl, but all of us. He means all the people God created and put here on this tiny planet in the middle of this vast universe. What is man? David says, "You (God) have made him a little lower than the angels, and crowned him with glory and honor." (KJV)

God made you and put you here. He made you different from every other creature and every other person in the universe. You can think and feel and decide what you want to do. He put you in charge of this incredible world and asks you to take care of it. He considers you just a little bit lower than the angels in heaven. He loves you and wants to be with you. He even became a man to show you just how much he loves you.

This mighty God who created the entire universe loves you. He thinks you are worth his complete attention. David said he crowns you with glory and honor. It's like his presence with you is a crown that marks you as royalty. Isn't that amazing? You are God's prince, his man, or God's princess, his handmaiden.

It's easy to look at the world around you and feel small. It's easy to look at the people around you and feel unimportant. The next time you're feeling like a nobody, remember this. God says you're somebody special. He's an awesome God!

Praise Project

Ask your mom or dad to let you go outside after dark or find a window that lets you see the night sky. Look up and try to count the stars. Think about how big the universe is. Remember the God who made it all thinks you are something special. Bring your Bible with you or write out Psalm 8 so you can sing the psalm to him as David did. He's awesome!

Because God Loves You

"I have loved you with an everlasting love; I have drawn you with loving kindness" (Jeremiah 31:3).

Once there was a young man whose father loved him very much. He worked on his father's land, caring for the vineyards and the animals, but he was restless. He was tired of working the land. He wanted to go out and see the world. He didn't have any money of his own, so he went to his father.

"Give me my share of the property," he said. "I want to get out of here, and I need money."

The father was sad. He didn't want to see the boy go. He knew what kind of trouble his young son might find in the places he wanted to go. His son wouldn't listen to him. He was determined to go, so the father gave him the inheritance.

The boy packed up his belongings and set off for a distant country. For a while, he lived well. He made friends who liked the way he spent money on them. He went to wild parties and acted important. He drank and gambled until his money was gone.

Then, a terrible famine came upon the land. Without any money, the boy couldn't buy even small bits of food. He finally found a job with a farmer, who gave him work feeding pigs. He was so hungry he would have eaten the slop the pigs ate, but no one would give him anything.

Finally the boy came to his senses. "Even the servants in my father's house have it better than this. They all have food to spare," he thought. "I'll go home."

The boy knew he had lost his place as a son. He had treated his father terribly, demanded his inheritance, and squandered it. He had lost everything. All the way back to his father's house, he rehearsed the words he would say. He went over and over them, desperate to find a way to survive. "I'll say: Father, I have sinned against heaven and against you. I'm not worthy to be called your son, but let me be a hired hand like your servants."

The boy trudged down the road. He clung to the hope that his father would not throw him out.

The boy's father often gazed down the road. He had never given up hope that his son would return, so he watched for him. While the boy was still a long way off, his father saw him. The old man's heart nearly burst with love. He ran down the road, threw his arms around his son, and kissed him.

The boy pulled away so he could say all the things he had practiced. "Father, I've sinned against you. I don't deserve to be your son."

But the old man paid no attention. He shouted to the servants, "Quick! Bring the best robe and put it on him. Put a ring on his finger and sandals on his feet. Bring the fattened calf and kill it. Let's have a feast to celebrate." He hugged the boy again. "This son of mine was dead, and now he is alive. He was lost, but now he's found." He pulled the boy into the house where the celebration was beginning.

Do you ever go your own way or do your own thing, like the boy in this story? God doesn't want you to go off and do your own thing. He wants you to live a healthy, holy life that is pleasing to him. He wants you to be in relationship with him.

God loves you. If you have walked away from God, he wants you to come home to him. The father in the story is a picture of how much God loves you. He is always watching for you to come back. He waits for you to return. His love never changes, no matter what you have done. He'll welcome you back into his arms.

Praise Project
God loves you. He loves you when you obey. He loves you when you don't, but he wants you to turn back to his way. If you have walked away from him, just turn around and tell God that you're sorry. God is just like the father in the story. Let him draw you close. Let him love you. Say thank you to him for loving you, even when you're stubborn and disobedient. Praise him for his wonderful love that draws you home.

Because God Chose You

You did not choose me, but I chose you (John 15:16).

Jesus had risen from the dead and ascended into heaven. His disciples were spreading the good news about Jesus' love all through Jerusalem and Judea. The church was growing, but not everyone was happy. The leaders of the Jews wanted to stop the disciples. They wanted to stop the church from growing. There was a terrible persecution of the church in Jerusalem.

A man named Saul was the worst. He went into house after house, dragging men and women off to jail. The believers in Christ left Jerusalem looking for a safe place to live and worship Jesus.

Saul went to the chief priest and got permission to go to Damascus and arrest anyone who believed in Jesus. He took soldiers with him and set off on the journey. They traveled for many days without any sign of the followers of Jesus. Dust from the road caked the travelers. As they approached Damascus, Saul must have looked forward to a meal and a good night's sleep.

Suddenly, a blinding light shone down on Saul. He swayed on his horse. Saul probably tried to grip the stirrups with his feet. Maybe he tried to hold the reins tighter, but he could not. He slipped off his horse and fell to the ground. Then he heard a voice.

"Saul, Saul, why are you persecuting me?" the voice said.

Saul must have struggled to rise. "Who are you, Lord?" he asked.

"I am Jesus, whom you persecute," the voice said.

Saul understood who it was that spoke to him. He must have trembled at the knowledge, but he lay still on the dusty road.

"Lord, what will you have me do?" he asked.

"Get up and go into the city. There I will tell you what you must do."

Saul sat up and tried to stand.

Soldiers came to help him. They had heard the noise, but they only saw Saul speaking. They tried to help him up, but it was clear as he rose that Saul was blind. The soldiers led him through the gates into the city.

Saul waited for three days in the house of a man named Judas. He didn't eat or drink. The soldiers stood guard over the house while Saul waited for God to tell him what to do.

There was a good man in Damascus, named Ananias. He was a believer in Jesus. One night, the Lord spoke to him in a vision. "Go to the street called Straight, to the house of Judas. Look for the man, Saul of Tarsus. He is praying to me."

Ananias must have trembled. Everyone knew that Saul was arresting Christians and throwing them in jail. Ananias also understood the mercy and love of God. He knew of God's forgiveness, but he was still terrified by the instructions.

"But Lord, I've heard about this man and all the evil he has done," Ananias said.

"Ananias," God said. "Go to him. I have chosen him to bring my name to the world."

Ananias could only obey. He set off down the narrow roads to find the house where Saul waited. When he reached the place, he entered the bedroom where Saul tossed and turned on the bed.

"Brother Saul," he said. "The Lord Jesus has sent me. The same one who appeared to you told me to come, so that you can see again."

Ananias laid his hands on Saul's eyes, and immediately something like scales fell from them, and Saul could see again. He got up from the bed and let Ananias baptize him. He could see the room, the sun shining through the window, the chair and table against the wall, the candle in its holder. He could see the face of Ananias. Saul was a new man, one chosen by God.

Saul, whose name was later changed to Paul, was the man God chose to share Jesus with the Gentiles, any people who were not of the Hebrew race. What a marvelous mission God gave him! Paul spent the rest of his life traveling all over the known world telling

people about Jesus. He endured beatings, shipwreck, and jail because of his love for Jesus. Churches grew because of his preaching. He wrote letters to his dear Christian friends. Many of these letters became part of the New Testament. Paul's calling gave him determination, courage, and joy.

God has called you too. Ephesians 2:10 says this. "For we are God's workmanship, created in Christ Jesus to do good works, which God prepared in advance for us to do." This means that God has a plan for you. He knows what he wants you to do. He has a plan for your life that will give you determination and joy, just as Paul's mission energized him.

Praise Project

You can be sure God has a plan for you, just like he had a plan for Paul. Do you wonder what destiny awaits you? Sometimes God speaks very clearly what he wants you to do. Sometimes he gives you a special talent or gift that he will use. Sometimes he gives you a desire to try a new idea or visit a new place. Sometimes he puts a person in your path to help to direct you. Praise God for choosing you. Tell him you're grateful for his love. Ask him to begin showing you his plan for your life.

Because God Created You

I praise you because I am fearfully and wonderfully made; your works are wonderful, I know that full well (Psalm 139:14).

God created every part of you. Before anyone set eyes on you, God knew just what you would look like. He decided if you would be a boy or a girl. He designed your hair color, your eyes and nose, your feet and your fingers. He decided how tall you would be and whether you would have big ears or small ones. He knew whether you would be a good runner or ballet dancer or a chess whiz.

God formed you while you were still in your mother's womb. The Bible says he wove you together, like someone making cloth or a basket. He put all the parts together—your bones and nerves, your muscles and tendons, your organs and skin—to make a complete, perfect person. He didn't make a single mistake.

When you were born, he was thrilled. He was proud of the way you looked. He was pleased with you. The Bible says he rejoices over you with joy, that you are fearfully and wonderfully made. Perfect, because he was the designer of *you*. You are a marvelous creation.

Because you are so special to him, God stays close by you. You are never out of his sight. His presence is always with you. You can't go anywhere to get away from God. If you climbed up to the sky, he would be there. If you dug deep under the ground, he would be there too. He even sees you in the dark. Daylight and dark are the same to him. He stays with you, his marvelous creation, and watches over you.

He knows when you sit down and when you get up. He knows when you go out to play and when you lie down to sleep. He knows what you are going to say even before

you say it. He knows what all the days of your life will be like. He watches you grow up and wants you to know him and love him and praise him.

God knows you better than anyone else. He knows your fears, your desires, and your hopes. He knows the very thoughts you think. He knows when you get upset or depressed. He knows when you think your body is too big or too small, when you think you're ugly or stupid. He always understands your thoughts, but he says again and again, that you are fearfully and wonderfully made. You are his wonderful creation.

It's important to believe what God says about you, because what he says is true. It's important to believe he made you, that he designed your body, your mind, and

your personality. When you look in the mirror, he wants you to see what he sees. He wants you to see his precious creation, his perfect work of art, his masterpiece. You!

If you believe what God says about you, you can do amazing things. You can stand up to peer pressure when you know God loves you and believes in you. You can walk away from sin when you know God is with you, giving you strength. You can be courageous and do the things he tells you to do, without fear, when you know he delights in you. You can truly be yourself when you know God loves the way he made you.

Praise Project

Celebrate your creation. Go outside and raise your hands to the sky. Praise God because he created you. Praise him because he made you perfectly. Praise him because he has designed you to do something that no one else can do, because no one else is made just like you. Praise him because you are fearfully and wonderfully made.

When you look in the mirror, never see yourself the same way again. Don't despise yourself or hate your body or the way you look. God says you are perfectly made. Praise him for your hair and your eyes and your body. Praise him. He thinks you're marvelous, and he's right.

Because God Provides For You

And my God will meet all your needs according to his glorious riches in Christ Jesus (Philippians 4:19).

Elijah was a prophet, a special messenger from God. God told him to speak to Ahab, the wicked king of Israel. Ahab did more to make God angry than any of the kings who came before him. He married the daughter of King Ethbaal, an enemy of Israel. He built a temple for foreign gods and worshipped them. God sent Elijah to confront Ahab.

"I serve the LORD God of Israel," Elijah said. "I promise you, there will be no rain until I say so. Total drought. Not even the dew will fall."

Ahab was in a rage. He wanted Elijah killed, but God told Elijah where to hide. "Head east and hide in the Kerith Ravine on the other side of the Jordan River," God said. "I have ordered the ravens to feed you, and you can drink water from the brook."

So Elijah went. He built himself a shelter in the ravine and lived there. He drank from the brook, and every morning and every evening the ravens brought him bread and meat. After a while, the grass turned brown.

The trees and shrubs wilted and died. The ground was hard and dry. The water in the brook flowed slower, until it was only a trickle. Then one day, it dried up completely. Elijah wondered what to do.

God spoke to him again. He said, "There's a woman in Zarephath. Go to her house. I've told her to feed you."

So Elijah went again. When he reached the city gates, he saw a woman gathering wood. "Please bring me a drink of water," he said to her. He was tired and dusty. He hadn't had anything to drink or eat since his journey began.

The woman turned without answering and went to fetch the water. As she was going, Elijah shouted at her, "And would you bring me something to eat too?"

At that, the woman turned around and came back. She looked at Elijah. Maybe she noticed his dirty feet or his tired eyes. Maybe she wanted to help, but she had lost all hope. "As surely as God lives," she said, "I don't have a single piece of bread. I have a handful of flour and a little oil. You found me gathering some sticks to take home and build a fire. I'll make one last meal for my son and me, one piece of bread. We'll eat it and then that will be all. We'll die."

Elijah rubbed his beard. He knew this was the woman God sent him to find. "Don't be afraid," he said. "Go ahead and make the bread, but first make a small piece of bread for me and bring it. Then make something for you and your son, because this is what God says: 'The jar of flour will not run out and the bottle of oil will not be empty until God sends rain on this land.'"

The woman made the bread for Elijah. She carried it to him and watched him eat the last of her supplies. Then she went back to her house, afraid there would be no flour, but wondering if God might do a miracle. She lifted the lid from the flour jar and looked in. It was full! Who could believe it? The bottle of oil was full too. The woman made a meal, not just a small piece of bread.

God's word to her proved true. The flour and oil lasted almost two years, until the drought was over. And Elijah

stayed with her until God sent him back to King Ahab with another message.

God provided for Elijah in an unusual way. He knew the hardship that Elijah would face in the drought. He knew that he needed food and water. No one knows where the ravens found the bread and meat, but they obeyed God, and Elijah didn't go hungry. When the drought became so severe that the brook dried up, God found another way to feed his prophet. It was a complete miracle.

God takes care of you. He knows what you need, and he meets those needs. He may not do it the way you expect or the way you think he should. He may use some pretty strange messengers, but he has promised to supply all your needs. Don't be afraid to tell him what you need. Watch for miracles to come when you least expect them.

Praise Project

Think of the ways God has provided for you. Do you have food, clothes, parents who love you, a school, a bed to sleep in at night? Take a minute and thank him for all he has already provided for you. Is there something else you need God to provide? Not just something you want, but something you really need. Does it seem like it would take a miracle? God is a God of miracles. Tell him what you need. Ask him to provide for you. He will. He does. Praise him.

Because God Rescues You

The LORD helps them and delivers them; he delivers them from the wicked and saves them, because they take refuge in him (Psalm 37:40).

Shadrach, Meshach and Abednego were slaves in Babylon. Nebuchadnezzar, who was the king of Babylon, had invaded Israel and carried away many Israelites from their home to serve him. Shadrach, Meshach and Abednego missed their home, but they served the king well. They were promoted to high positions in Nebuchadnezzar's kingdom.

One day, King Nebuchadnezzar built a gold statue. It was ninety feet high, about as tall as a ten-story building today. The king ordered all the important officials to come to a grand ceremony to dedicate the statue. Shadrach, Meshach and Abednego went.

As the crowd gathered in front of the statue, a herald shouted. "Attention, people of every nation and language," he said. "This is what you are commanded to do. When you hear the sound of the horn, flute, harp, lyre, and psaltery, you must fall to your knees and worship the gold statue. Anyone who doesn't will be thrown into a blazing furnace."

When the instruments played, everyone fell down and worshipped. They didn't want to be thrown into the fire. Everyone obeyed Nebuchadnezzar's order, except Shadrach, Meshach and Abednego. They refused to worship anything except Jehovah, the one true God.

When the king's fortune tellers saw the three friends still standing, they went to the king. "You gave strict orders, O king, for everyone to worship the statue. But these Jews are not obeying. They won't worship your gods."

Nebuchadnezzar was furious. He had the three men brought to him. "Is this true?" he demanded. "I'll give you

one more chance. When you hear the horn, flute, harp, lyre, and psaltery, fall down and worship the image I have made. If you don't, I'll have you thrown into the furnace. What god can rescue you from my power?"

Shadrach, Meshach and Abednego refused. "If you throw us into the fire, the God we serve is able to save us. But we want you to know, O king, that even if he doesn't, we will not bow down to your gods."

Nebuchadnezzar was so angry, he had the furnace heated seven times hotter than usual. He commanded strong soldiers to tie the three friends up and throw them into the furnace. Shadrach, Meshach and Abednego fell into the blazing fire.

Suddenly, King Nebuchadnezzar jumped up.

"Didn't we throw three men into the fire, bound hand and foot?" he asked.

"That's right," they answered him.

"Look! There are four men, walking around unbound, in the fire. They're unharmed. And the fourth man looks like a son of the gods."

Nebuchadnezzar went to the door of the furnace and shouted, "Shadrach, Meshach and Abednego, servants of the Most High God. Come here. Come out."

So the three friends came out of the fire, and all the king's counselors crowded around them. They saw the fire had not harmed them. Not a hair was scorched. Their clothes weren't burned. They didn't even smell like smoke.

"Blessed be the God of Shadrach, Meshach and Abednego!" the king said. "Their God sent an angel and rescued his servants who trusted in him. They defied my orders and were willing to die rather than serve another god. From now on, no one will speak against the God of Shadrach, Meshach and Abednego. No other god can save anyone like this."

Shadrach, Meshach and Abednego had faith. They defied a king that commanded them to do something wrong. They believed that God would save them, but if he didn't, they still refused to bow down to Nebuchadnezzar's idol. What did God do? He sent the angel of the LORD to walk with them in the fire. Some people believe it was Jesus himself who came to be with them. God rescued them in a mighty way.

Think though. When did he save them? It was *while* they were in the fire. He didn't stop the king's soldiers from throwing them in the furnace. But while they were in the middle of this hard challenge, he came and walked with them, and he protected them from harm.

God doesn't always keep you from facing difficulty, but he always walks with you right in the middle of it.

Praise Project

Are you in the middle of a difficult situation? Maybe you feel like you're in the fiery furnace. Use your imagination. It's a wonderful tool God created for you to use to see him. Picture God holding your hand, and putting his arm around you, and helping you through it all. Receive his comfort. Listen to his voice. Praise him. He's with you in the fire. He will come and rescue you too. Sing a song to him.

Because God Comforts You

As a mother comforts her child, so will I comfort you (Isaiah 66:13).

Remember David and his battle with the giant, Goliath? All the soldiers of Israel watched as David killed the giant. Jonathan, King Saul's son, was impressed by David's skill and courage. The two boys, who were about the same age, became best friends.

King Saul continued to fight with the Philistines, even after Goliath was dead. Jonathan was a brave soldier and fought with his father's armies, but one day the battle went badly. King Saul and Jonathan were both killed. The Philistines celebrated their victory while David grieved for the loss of his king and his dear friend.

The people soon made David their new king. David spent many years fighting against the Philistines and other enemies of Israel. Finally, the wars were over and there was peace. David had time to rest. He remembered his friend, Jonathan, and the good times they shared. He remembered a promise he once made, a promise that he would care for Jonathan's family.

David called for the nobles of his palace. "God has been kind to me. Is there anyone left of the family of Saul? Are any of Jonathan's children alive that I can show kindness to?"

They told David about one of Saul's servants, named Ziba. Ziba cared for Saul's farm in the country. He had managed it well and had become a wealthy man.

David called for Ziba. He asked his question again. "Is anyone in Saul's family still alive?"

"Saul's son, Jonathan, had a little boy, named Mephibosheth. He's a grown man now and living at Lo Debar, but he's lame."

Mephibosheth was just a child when the news came that Saul and Jonathan were dead. The boy's nurse was afraid the Philistines would look for any relatives of Saul that might become king after him. She picked the boy up and ran from the house. She fled into the countryside. In her hurry to hide, she tripped and fell on top of Mephibosheth. The boy's feet were injured.

The nurse carried him across the Jordan River. She rubbed medicinal creams on him and comforted the boy, but his feet would not heal. Mephibosheth grew up lame. They stayed in that far place across the Jordan. Once David was king, the nurse was afraid he might want to get rid of Mephibosheth. Kings did that in those days when they took power from another king.

When David heard the story, he didn't waste a minute. He sent for Mephibosheth.

Mephibosheth arrived at the palace. He limped into the throne room and bowed low to the king.

"Mephibosheth?" David asked.

"Yes, my lord. I am your servant." Mephibosheth's voice trembled.

"Don't be afraid," David said. "I loved your father, Jonathan, and I want to do something to remember him. I'm going to give you all the land that belonged to your grandfather, Saul. And from now on, you'll eat all your meals at my table with me."

Mephibosheth couldn't believe his ears. He shuffled his lame feet and stammered, "Who am I that you would pay attention to a stray dog like me?"

David ignored his outburst. He called Ziba, Saul's servant and told him the news. "You and your sons and servants will farm the land and bring in the crops, so that Jonathan's family will be provided for. But Mephibosheth will eat his meals here with me."

So Mephibosheth moved to Jerusalem. He ate with King David, like one of the king's own sons.

David's kindness brought comfort to Mephibosheth. He had lived all his life hidden away, crippled, and probably lonely. Now he was accepted as part of the

king's family. He married and had a son of his own. He wasn't alone anymore.

Mephibosheth's presence at David's table probably brought comfort to David too. Whenever he remembered his friend and felt sad about Jonathan's death, he could look down the table and see Jonathan's son.

God knows his children need to be comforted. He says he comforts you just like a mother comforts her child. How does he do that? Sometimes he sends real people to put real arms around you. When you're sick, your mom holds a cold wash cloth to your face. That's comfort. When you're upset, a friend puts his arm around you. That's comfort. God puts people in your life that can comfort you.

God also gives you the Holy Spirit. When you become a Christian, the Holy Spirit comes to live in you. In John 14–16, Jesus described the Holy Spirit as the comforter. He said the Holy Spirit would help you remember what Jesus said. No matter what happens to you, you can always ask the Holy Spirit to comfort you, to remind you what Jesus would say, to speak just the right words to help you feel better.

Praise Project

Do you need comfort? Talk to God about it. Tell him what's bothering you. Ask the Holy Spirit to comfort you. Close your eyes and imagine God picking you up and holding you close. Remind him of his promise to comfort you. Praise him because he knows you need comfort and he provides it. Say thank you.

Because God is Faithful to You

Know therefore that the LORD *your God is God; he is the faithful God, keeping his covenant of love to a thousand generations of those who love him and keep his commands (Deuteronomy 7:9).*

Joseph was next to the youngest of Jacob's twelve sons. He was a dreamer and his father's favorite. His ten older brothers were jealous. One night Joseph dreamed he and his brothers were binding up the grain in the field. Suddenly Joseph's sheaf of grain stood up. His brother's sheaves bowed down to his. Joseph believed the dreams were true. He believed God had sent the dreams to him, but he wasn't very wise. He bragged about the dream to his brothers, and they began to hate him.

Joseph had another dream. This time the sun and the moon and the stars bowed down to him. Joseph still hadn't learned to keep his dreams to himself. He told his brothers this one too, and they hated him more. Even his father rebuked him. How could he believe his mother and father and all his brothers would bow down to him?

The brothers were so angry, they plotted to get rid of him. When Joseph came looking for them, they threw him into a pit and sold him to slave traders, who were on their way to Egypt. The brothers killed a goat and smeared the blood on Joseph's coat. They told their father the boy must have died. The old man grieved. The brothers knew Joseph wasn't dead, but they never told.

Joseph became a slave in the house of Potiphar in Egypt. He was a cheerful worker and he learned quickly. God was with Joseph and helped him succeed in everything he did. Before long, Potiphar put Joseph in charge of all his household affairs. God blessed Potiphar's house because of Joseph.

Potiphar's wife was friendly at first. Then she became too friendly. Joseph was strong and handsome, but he was also faithful to his master. When Joseph wouldn't kiss her, she screamed and tore his robe. She made up a story about how wicked Joseph had been. Potiphar believed his wife and had Joseph thrown into jail.

God was with Joseph in the prison too. The warden watched Joseph. He saw that everything Joseph did went well. Before long, Joseph was put in charge of all the prisoners. One day, the king's cupbearer and his baker were brought down to the jail. The captain of the guard assigned Joseph to watch over them. They hadn't been there too long when each man had a dream. Joseph knew about dreams. He asked God to tell him what the two men's dreams meant, and God did.

In the cupbearer's dream, three vines budded and bore fruit. A hand crushed the grapes and gave the wine to Pharaoh. Joseph told him in three days he would be restored to his job. The baker's dream was not so happy. Three baskets of bread sat on his head, and birds pecked at the bread. Joseph told him that in three days Pharaoh would chop off his head. And that's exactly what happened.

Joseph begged the cupbearer to remember him when he came back to his post, but the man forgot. By the time this happened Joseph had been a slave for about ten years. That was a long time to wait for God's promise to redeem him. And what about those dreams? How could anyone bow down to him? He was a prisoner in a dungeon.

Two more years passed. One day Pharaoh had a dream. A terrible dream. He was standing by the Nile River when seven sleek, fat cows came out of the river to graze. Then seven ugly, scrawny cows came out of the river and ate the healthy cows. Pharaoh tried to go back to sleep, but he had the same terrible dream again. This time seven thin, scorched heads of grain ate up seven healthy heads of grain.

No one could tell Pharaoh what the dreams meant. That's when the cupbearer remembered Joseph. They cleaned Joseph up and brought him to Pharaoh. God told Joseph what the dreams meant. There would be seven good years with good crops. Then there would be seven years of famine. Joseph told Pharaoh to find someone to store up grain while the harvest was good, so that when the famine came, there would be food in the land.

Who did Pharaoh appoint? Right. He appointed Joseph. Joseph managed the harvest well. When the famine came, he had stored enough grain for all the people in Egypt.

The famine was all over, not just in Egypt. There was famine back in Joseph's home too. Jacob and his sons and grandchildren were running out of food, so Jacob sent the brothers to Egypt. Joseph was in charge of selling the grain. He saw his brothers come and bow down to him, asking to buy grain. They didn't know him, but Joseph recognized them. And remembered his dreams.

What does it mean to be faithful? God's faithfulness has to do with keeping his covenant of love. Faithfulness and love are often tied together in the Bible. God keeps his promises because he loves his people. He is always faithful to love them and care for them. Even when Joseph was a slave and wondered if God had forgotten him, God was still faithful. Joseph just couldn't see the whole picture.

Praise Project

God is faithful to all his promises. He made you and he loves you. The Bible says the steadfast love of the LORD never ceases. His mercy never ends. Every sunrise brings with it new evidence of his faithfulness. Has God given you a promise? Remind him of it in your prayers. Praise him for being a faithful God, for never changing in his love toward you, for keeping his promises.

Made to Praise

Praise the LORD. Praise, O servants of the LORD, praise the name of the LORD (Psalm 113:1).

Have you ever had a challenging teacher or a tough coach that you liked and respected? Maybe that teacher required more from you than you thought you could give, but you worked hard because you wanted to please them. Or maybe your coach demanded physical endurance that you didn't know you had, but you dropped to the ground and did the pushups because you wanted the coach to be proud of you. You worked harder than ever before, not because the teacher threatened you with punishment, but because you admired, respected, and loved them.

When God says to praise, he wants you to respond that same way to him. He wants you to praise because you love him and respect him, because you want him to be proud of you. He wants you to do what he says because you choose his way over your own.

All through the Bible, God tells his people to praise him. The laws he gave to Moses commanded an offering of praise. Isaiah said, "Sing to the LORD a new song, his praise from the ends of the earth." Jeremiah said, "Sing to the LORD! Give praise to the LORD!" Nehemiah said, "Stand up and praise the LORD your God, who is from everlasting to everlasting."

Even Jesus praised God. He said, "I praise you, Father, LORD of heaven and earth, because you have hidden these things from the wise and learned, and revealed them to little children." (Matt. 11:25) Jesus knew that adults can get so busy and so complicated in their reasoning, they forget the important things. Things like praise. He knew that often children understood and believed his words more easily than the adults.

Jesus loved it when children were around him. One day a crowd of people pressed around him. Some wanted to be healed, some wanted to hear his words, some just wanted to see this man that the whole countryside was talking about. The disciples tried their best to keep some order, to keep Jesus from being crushed.

A group of mothers pushed through the crowd. Some carried babies. Others grasped young children by the hand and pulled them closer to Jesus. When the disciples saw all the children, they tried to send them away. They knew the sick people needed Jesus, but

127

there were just too many people this day for him to be bothered with children. "Go on home," they said. "Jesus doesn't have time. Can't you see this crowd of people?"

The mothers just pushed harder, as they edged through the crowd. Then Jesus looked up. When he saw the disciples trying to send the children away, he was upset with them. "Don't send them away. Let them come to me," he said.

So they came. The children surrounded Jesus. They probably tugged on his robe, hugged his legs, and begged to be picked up. Jesus lifted them up in his strong arms and asked his Father to bless them.

On another day, when Jesus was in the temple in Jerusalem healing the sick, the children caught sight of him. They watched him heal blind and lame people. They ran around the temple courtyard shouting, "Hosanna to the Son of David!"

The chief priests and the teachers at the temple were offended. "Do you hear what these children are saying?" they asked him.

"Yes," Jesus answered, "Haven't you read the scripture? It says, 'From the lips of children and infants God has ordained praise?'"

That's right. God has designed you to praise, no matter how old you are. He says to praise. Be obedient because you love him. Praise the Lord.

Praise Project

Have you found a favorite way of praising God? Maybe you enjoy praise in song. Sing a song to him. If you enjoy dancing, then dance for him. Everything you do should be done for God's glory. Do you like to shout your praise? Shout your love to him. Do you feel like you can reach out and almost touch him when you raise your hands? Then lift your hands to him in praise. Do you feel quiet tonight? Kneel down and thank him for loving you. Jesus said, "If you love me, you will keep my commandments." Do you love him? Praise him.

Even the Trees Rejoice

The heavens declare the glory of God; the skies proclaim the work of his hands (Psalm 19:1).

In the beginning, God created everything. He set the heavens in place. He made the sun and the stars, the ocean and the land, the fish and the birds, the plants and flowers, and Adam and Eve. All of creation shows his mighty power.

On the seventh day after God created the world, he rested. He took the time to look at everything he had

made and to see that it was good. He stopped his work and enjoyed the valleys and mountains, the rivers and streams. Maybe he watched squirrels playing in the trees or bears wrestling in the forest. Maybe he rejoiced to see salmon leaping upstream or flowers blowing in the wind. God was pleased with his creation. It reflected his glory.

Did you know that humans are not the only ones that praise God? It's true. The psalms talk about all creation praising him. The whole earth is glad that he is the king. The mountains and hills break forth into singing. The fields are jubilant. Fruit trees and cedars praise his name. The sea and all that's in it resounds with praises. The rivers clap their hands. Wild animals and cattle, small creatures and flying birds praise the Lord.

The heavens rejoice. The highest heavens and the waters above the skies, lightning and hail, snow and clouds, even the stormy winds praise him. The sun and the moon praise him and all the shining stars. It was a star that led the wise men to Jesus.

Jesus knew that creation shouted its own praise to God. Near the end of his ministry on the earth, he planned to go to Jerusalem. He knew he was heading toward death and the cross, but he determined to finish what God had sent him to do.

He sent two of his disciples to a nearby village. "You will find a colt tied there that no one has ever ridden. Untie it and bring it here. If anyone asks what you're doing, tell them the Lord needs it, and I will send it back to them soon."

The two disciples went and found the colt. As they untied it, some people standing by asked what they were doing. The disciples answered with the words Jesus had given them, and the people let them take the colt. They brought the colt to Jesus. Before he climbed up, the disciples laid their cloaks across its back for Jesus to sit on. Then they went to Jerusalem.

By this time in his ministry, Jesus had healed many, many people. He had cast out demons. He had told the people stories about God. He had raised Lazarus from the dead. He was famous all over the country.

When the people heard he was coming, they ran out to see him. Some rushed in front of the colt and laid their cloaks on the ground. Some people cut palm branches and laid them on the road too. There were so many cloaks and branches; it must have looked like a royal carpet rolled out for a king to ride on.

People lined the roadway. They shouted and sang, "Hosanna! Blessed is the king who comes in the name of the Lord! Hosanna in the highest!"

Some of the Pharisees in the crowd didn't like what was happening. They called out to Jesus. "Teacher, get your disciples under control!"

Jesus knew what the Pharisees were thinking. He knew they were plotting to have him arrested. He knew they didn't know who he was or why the people praised him, but Jesus understood. He looked at the Pharisees. "I tell you, if they kept quiet, the stones would shout praises."

Jesus understood that nature praises God.

Praise Project

Spend some time observing God's creation. Look at the stars. Pick a flower or a leaf and study it closely. Praise God for the beauty of creation. Make a list of all the things in nature that you are thankful for. Read your list to God and tell him what a wonderful creator he is. Praise him for his wonderful works.

Heaven's Praise

Praise him, all his angels, praise him, all his heavenly hosts (Psalm 148:2).

An old man named John lived on an island called Patmos. Some people think this John is the same man who was Jesus' disciple, who wrote the gospel of John, and who healed the lame man with Peter. They believe the Roman emperor banished John to the island as punishment for preaching about Jesus.

John lived, worked, and worshipped on the small island off the coast of Greece. One Sunday John was praying. Suddenly he heard a loud, clear voice behind him. When he turned, he saw a vision. A door opened in heaven, and a voice said, "Come up to this place."

John was immediately taken up into heaven, and he saw the throne of God. He could hardly see the one sitting on the throne because the glory around him was so great. Twenty-four old men, the elders of the church, sat on thrones around him. They wore gold crowns. There was a rainbow over the throne.

Lightning and thunder came from the throne of God. In front of the throne, there was a sea, clear as glass. Beside the throne, four strange living creatures with six wings each praised God continually. They never took a break, day or night. They said, "Holy, holy, holy is the Lord God, Almighty, who was and is and is to come."

Then the elders fell down before God and laid their crowns at his feet. They worshipped him, saying, "You are worthy, O God, to have all the honor and glory and power, for you created all things."

Then John saw a book rolled up like a scroll in the hands of the one on the throne. An angel stood up and asked, "Who is worthy to open the book?" John began to weep, because there was no one who could open it.

The twenty-four elders spoke to John, "Don't weep. The Lion of Judah has won the right to open the book."

Then John saw Jesus, standing before the throne, the same Jesus who had been killed on the cross for sinners. He came to the one on the throne and took the book. Then the four creatures and the twenty-four elders worshipped him. They all sang a new song. "You are worthy to take up the scroll and to open it because you were slain. Because with your blood, you purchased men for God."

John looked around heaven. He saw thousands and thousands of angels. Ten thousands of angels. They sang, "Worthy is the Lamb, who was slain, to receive power and wealth and wisdom and strength and honor and glory and praise!"

Then John heard every creature in heaven and on earth and under the earth and in the sea. They all sang the song praising God, worshipping him.

John wrote his vision in the book of Revelations so everyone could have a picture of the worship in heaven. John wasn't the only one who saw into the heavens. When Nehemiah dedicated the temple, he praised God for the multitudes of heaven that worshipped him. God came and talked to Job. He told Job how the angels shouted for joy at the creation of the world.

Isaiah had a vision of the winged creatures around the throne. He heard them singing, "Holy, holy, holy is the Lord." When the angel spoke to the shepherds outside Bethlehem, suddenly a great host of angels joined in to praise God. When Jesus told the story of the lost son who wasted his inheritance, he reminded his listeners that the angels in heaven rejoiced when one sinner came home to God.

Praise Project

Choose one of the songs John heard the angels and the elders sing. Read it to yourself a few times. Can you make it into a song? Sing your song to God. All the hosts of heaven will sing with you.

A Life of Praise

*I will sing unto the L*ORD *as long as I live: I will sing praise to my God while I have my being (Psalm 104:33 KJV).*

When Jesus was eight days old, Mary and Joseph took him to the temple. It was the custom in those days for the parents to offer a sacrifice and dedicate the child to God. So the little family packed up their donkey and headed for Jerusalem. The journey was only five miles from Bethlehem. The road wound up and down over rocky hills. Mary would have been sitting on the donkey holding the tiny baby in her arms.

When they reached Jerusalem, Joseph probably found a stable for the donkey. He took Mary by the arm, and with the baby Jesus, they walked up the stone steps into the temple. Tall columns held up the ancient building. Incense perfumed the air. The first person they met was Simeon.

Simeon was a good man who loved God. God had made him a promise. He told Simeon that he would not die before he saw the Messiah. So Simeon waited and prayed. The Holy Spirit prompted him to go to the temple this very day. He was there when Mary and Joseph entered with Jesus. Simeon knew immediately this was the Messiah. He took the baby into his arms and praised God. "I've seen your salvation with my own eyes. He's a light that will lead all people everywhere to God."

Mary and Joseph were amazed. They turned to go, but before they could reach the altar for their sacrifice, an old woman stopped them. Anna was eighty-four. She had been a widow for a long, long time. She came to the temple every day. She spent her whole life worshipping and praising God. Like Simeon, Anna recognized Jesus. She knew he was the promised Messiah who would bring freedom to his people. Anna thanked God for sending Jesus. She kept on thanking him and telling everyone in the temple about Jesus.

Both Simeon and Anna praised God all their lives. Their praises taught them to hear God's voice and to sense his presence. They were attuned to what God was doing. So when Jesus came, they recognized him. They praised God for his gift to them and to everyone.

David lived a life of praise too. He was determined to praise God no matter what happened to him, no matter where he was, and no matter how he felt. As long as he had breath, he made a conscious choice to praise. And like Simeon and Anna, he was tuned in to God. He heard God speak to him and knew God's presence was with him.

As a young boy, he sang songs of praise in the fields while he watched over the sheep. As a young man, he shouted praise for God's help in battle. As a young king, he danced for joy to celebrate God's presence. When he made wrong choices, he bowed down and thanked God for bringing him back to the right path. He designed and built musical instruments to praise God. He wrote down instructions for how the choirs and orchestras should praise in the tabernacle and the temple. As an old man, he commended God to his son. Praise him, he told Solomon. Always, praise him.

David would say the same words to you today. He would remind you that God inhabits your praises. If

you want to hear God's voice when he speaks, then praise. If you want to see his deliverance in your life, then praise. If you want to sense his presence with you, then praise. Praise in the morning when you wake up and at night when you go to bed. Praise when you feel great and when you feel lousy. Praise when you see a beautiful sunset. Raise your hands to the sky and praise like the trees of the field. Sing like David sang.

Praise Project

Let the words of David be the story of your life. In Psalm 27 he said, "One thing I ask of the LORD, this is what I seek: that I may dwell in the house of the LORD all the days of my life." David didn't mean he wanted to stay in church all the time. He wanted to stay in God's presence all the time. And praise helped him stay there.

Use the praise tools you've learned. Choose the ones that help you come into the presence of God, and use them daily. Pray David's prayer. Praise him. Make your life a life of praise.

Words and their pronunciation

Yadah - (Pronounced *yaw-daw'*)

Halal - (Pronounced *haw-lal'*)

Gadal - (Pronounced *gaw-dal'*)

Towdah - (Pronounced *to-daw'*)

Tehillah - (Pronounced *teh-hil-law'*)

Zamar - (Pronounced *zaw-mar'*)

Ruwa - (Pronounced *roo-ah'*)

Shabach - (Pronounced *shaw-bakh'*)

Barak - (Pronounced *baw-rak'*)

Raqad - (Pronounced *raw-kad'*)

The Singing Soldiers
by Barbara Haley
ISBN: 978-1-84550-249-2

You wouldn't send a choir into a battle? Would you set up a sing-song in a stinking old jail? What would you cheer about if your enemy and all his chariots had just gone belly up in the Red Sea? Could you sing a cranky old king out of his bad mood? And what about when you've just lost everything you've ever loved and singing must be the last thing on your mind? Well, each one of these situations is a real life story in the Bible and in this book. Winston doesn't have to battle with a choir, but he does have to deal with his freaky aunt Frieda. Avery hasn't been chucked into prison but she discovers that people in jail do like to sing - and that even she can be a bit *off-pitch* sometimes. Natalie isn't watching any chariots drown, but her little brother teaches her that God is awesome. Mike is the one who is cranky and bored, but he finds out that God's got plans! And when Danielle doesn't feel like singing, she finds that there are others worse off and that she can always tell God how wonderful he is.

CHRISTIAN FOCUS PUBLICATIONS

Christian Focus | Christian Heritage | CF4K | Mentor

Christian Focus Publications publishes books for adults and children under its four main imprints: Christian Focus, Christian Heritage, CF4K and Mentor. Our books reflect that God's word is reliable and Jesus is the way to know him, and live for ever with him.

Our children's publication list includes a Sunday school curriculum that covers pre-school to early teens; puzzle and activity books. We also publish personal and family devotional titles, biographies and inspirational stories that children will love.

If you are looking for quality Bible teaching for children then we have an excellent range of Bible story and age specific theological books.

From pre-school to teenage fiction, we have it covered!

Find us at our web page:
www.christianfocus.com

CF4·K
Because you're never
too young to know Jesus